WHO'S WHO
IN NEW PULP

AIRSHIP 27 PRODUCTIONS

Who's Who in New Pulp
© 2020 Airship 27 Productions

Published by Airship 27 Productions
www.airship27.com
www.airship27hangar.com

Interior illustrations © 2020 each artist as listed
Cover illustration © 2020 Rob Davis

Editor: Ron Fortier
Associate Editor: Jonathan Sweet
Production designer: Rob Davis
Promotions Manager: Michael Vance

ISBN: 978-1-946183-83-5

Printed in the United States of America

10 9 8 7 6 5 4 3 2 1

WHO'S WHO IN NEW PULP

Dedicated to

Tom & Ginger Johnson - Robert & Phyllis Weinberg
The bridge builders who paved the way here.

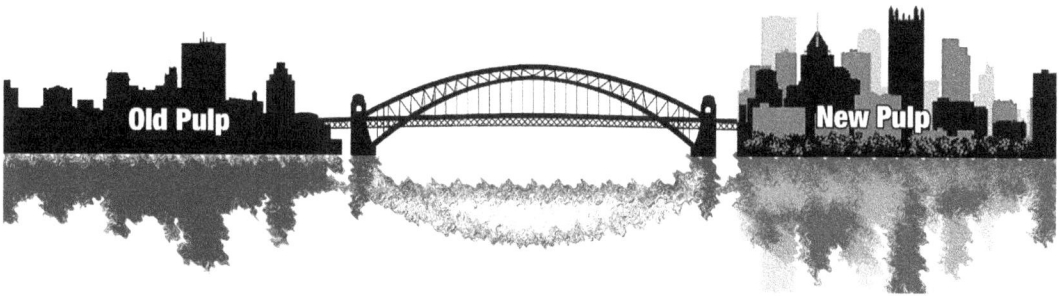

Old Pulp

New Pulp

ADAMS JR., FRED
Born—13 Sept 1949
112 Sabra Court
Uniontown, PA 15401

website: drphreddee.com
E-mail:drphredde@atlanticbb.net

Writer—Editor—Proofreader—Instructor

Retired English faculty, Penn State University; published author, fiction and nonfiction, since 1971. Creator of series characters: Hitwolf, Six Gun Terrors, C.O. Jones, The Smith Brothers, Ike Mars, Sam Dunne and Featherstone of Lloyd's. Three-time nominee for Best Pulp Novel in the Pulp Factory Awards; Associate Editor for Airship 27 Productions.

ALEXANDER, P.
Born—1984
PO Box 56023
Little Rock, AR 72215
United States of America

website: www.cirsova.wordpress.com
E-mail: (cirsova@yahoo.com)

Editor—Publisher—Reviewer—Writer

"Alex" P. Alexander is best known as the editor and owner of Cirsova Publishing and the publisher of Cirsova Magazine, Michael Tierney's Wild Stars, and Jim Breyfogle's Tales of the Mongoose and Meerkat. Cirsova's flagship publication, Cirsova Magazine, was a 2017 Hugo Award finalist for Best Semi-Pro Zine. Not necessarily part of the "New Pulp" scene, Alexander was involved with a dissident faction of the OSR emerging in the mid-2010s that was focusing on a return to "Appendix N"-style fiction, with his focus particularly on 40s and 50s pulps [Planet Stories especially]. Blogger and culture commentator Daddy Warpig described this activity as "the Pulp Revolution." In 2019, Alexander published a "lost" Edgar Rice Burroughs Tarzan story based on a fragment posthumously completed by Michael Tierney. He's written a branching-path novella, some OSR TTRPG content, and published a handful of short stories under pseudonyms. For a few years, he reviewed classic pulp stories at Castalia House, but now publishes them on his own site. He even had a short pro-gig reviewing abandonware video games. In another life, he played in some terrible punk and industrial bands that you probably would not enjoy.

ALEXANDER, TERRY
Born - 27th, August 1954
29712 S. 75th St. E.
Porum, Ok. 74455
Unites States of America

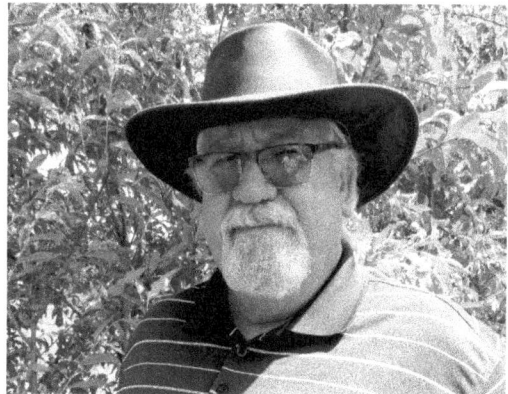

E-mail: terryale@crosstel.net

Writer

Terry Alexander and his wife Phyllis live on a small farm near Porum, Oklahoma.

They have a small cow and calf operation. They have three children, thirteen grandchildren and four great grandchildren. Terry is a member of Oklahoma Writers Federation Inc. Ozark Creative Writers, and Tahlequah Writers. Terry has been published in several anthologies from Airship 27, Pro Se Productions, Moonstone Books, Big Pulp, and several others. He writes a column for Saddlebag Dispatches which is published by OGHMA Creative Media and a column in Midnight Magazine by Man Cave Entertainment.

ANDERSON, KEVIN J.

Born—27 March 1962
PO Box 1840
Monument CO 80132
United States of America

(Photo by T. Duren Jones.)

website: www.wordfire.com
E-mail: (readers@wordfire.com)

Writer—Editor—Publisher

Bestselling, prolific genre writer of science fiction, fantasy, horror, best known for his continuation of the Dune series with Brian Herbert, his steampunk fantasy collaborations with Neil Peart (legendary drummer from rock band Rush), and his novels in the Star Wars, X-Files, Batman and Superman universes. His most popular original works are the space epic Saga of Seven Suns and Saga of Shadows, epic fantasy trilogies Terra Incognita and Wake the Dragon, and his humorous horror series featuring Dan Shamble, Zombie P.I. Along with his wife, bestselling author Rebecca Moesta, Anderson is the publisher of WordFire Press, with over 350 titles and 100 authors. He is also a professor and director of the Publishing MA program at Western Colorado University.

ANDERSON, RUSS JR.

Born—17 Oct 1974
Baltimore, MD
United States of America

E-mail: russlee74@gmail.com

Writer—Editor—Publisher

Pulp writer/editor, best known for editing the HOW THE WEST WAS WEIRD anthologies. He was also the original editor/publisher of Derrick Ferguson's Dillon and the Voice of Odin. As a writer, he has contributed multiple stories to various Pro Se and Airship 27 anthologies. His novels include MYTHWORLD (a modern, magical realist take on Greek myth), THE VENGEFUL CORPSE (a 1950s crime thriller starring a masked female crimefighter), and the AUBREY ARTHUR series (a young adult, urban fantasy series). He once won a spelling bee in grade school... but he's pretty sure it was rigged.

ANGELO, JR., RALPH L.

Born - July 27th, 1959
24 S. Kennedy Dr.

Centereach, NY 11720
United States of America

website http://RLAngeloJr.com
E-mail:-RLAngeloJr@gmail.com

Writer—Editor—Publisher - Reviewer

New Pulp/Sci-Fi adventure author best known for 'The Cagliostro Chronicles', 'Hyperforce', 'Redemption of the Sorcerer', 'Torhag the Warrior', The Grim Spectre' and many more!
Ralph was awarded 'Best New Author' for the 'New Pulp Awards' in 2014.
Ralph is currently writing the next chapter of 'The Cagliostro Chronicles' series which will be followed by the next Hyperforce novel.
Ralph's hobbies include guitar, motorcycles, martial arts, and skiing, with a little online gaming thrown in there as well.

AQUILONE, JAMES
Born - July 1973
Staten Island, NY
United States of America

websites—jamesaquilone.com, deadjack.com
E-mail: (jamesaquilone@gmail.com)

Writer—Editor

Writer and editor is best known for his Dead Jack series of fantasy/horror stories. The first novel in the zombie P.I. series, *Dead Jack and the Pandemonium Device*, has been optioned for TV and film. His short fiction has been published in such markets as Nature Magazine, *The Best of Galaxy's Edge 2013-2014*, and *Unidentified Funny Objects 4*. He is the Managing Editor of Weird Tales Magazine.

AUFFHAMMER, TYLER
Born—28 Nov 1992
North Carolina
United States of America

E-mail: (ttauffhammer@gmail.com)

Writer

Tyler Auffhammer's first New Pulp publication was *1950s Western Roundup* (Pro Se Productions, 2018), a western anthology that features real-life outlaws "whitewashed" into lovable heroes. Auffhammer's sampling, "Ace Up His Sleeve", centers around gambler and outlaw John "King" Fisher. He followed that up with a man-against-nature story, "Edge of the Abyss", published in *Crimson Streets* later that year. His next publication, *Marshal Horne of Talon's Crossing*, is a western anthology debuting in 2020 from Airship 27 Productions. Auffhammer has also worked for Steeger Books (formerly

Altus Press) as a blurb writer. He graduated from Western Carolina University in 2015 and teaches English & Creative Writing in North Carolina.

BAKER, ROCK
Born - 3 Nov 1981
United States of America

website - https://rock-baker.blogspot.com/
E-mail: - rockbaker1981@gmail.com

Writer - Artist

Cartoonist best known for AC Comics' Femforce, in which appeared his original strip, Dinosaur Girl. Also the strip Betsy The Bookwriter and the graphic novel DAHL for Main Enterprises. Also published in Bloke's Terrible Tomb of Terror and Moonstone's Domino Lady Vs The Mummy. Currently writing/drawing Cartoon Cuties for InDELLible. This project involves both comic book and literary adventures concerning glamorous cartoon characters living in 1950's Hollywood.

BANE, TIMOTHY
Born—13 Oct 1971
28 College Circle, Staunton, VA 24401
United States of America

E-mail: (admin@scaldcrow.com)

Creative Director—Artist—Writer—Publisher

Bane is best known for his work on Scaldcrow Games, RPG products and Little Buck's Fantastic Visions (illustrations). He was also the creative director for NeDeo Press, winning the PMA's Benjamin Franklin Award in 2006, for his book design, illustration, and layout of "Ivy Cole and the Moon," by Gina Farago. He is the founder and director of Scaldcrow Games since 2008.

BARNARD, MARK
Born—31 August 1953
Kansas
United States of America
E-mail: (aztecmummy@hotmail.com)

Writer-Artist-Graphics Designer

Writer OPERATION: DEEP SPACE (radio anthology series) and writer/artist for the independent comic BETTLE MECHA LONE BLUE. Worked for several years as an inker on various independent comic book series before transitioning to scripting. Over 50 credits in the comics field as writer, artist or inker. Possibly best known for the space-opera spoof HAVOC, INC, and LARK & KEY, which ran in a British anthology title. Currently writing three continuing pulp series—THE MAN WITH THE GREEN EYES, TALES OF THE RED ACE and ALIAS THE ECLIPSE, as well as the humorous sci-fi detective series WILDER & GEL, LLC. Has had two stories printed by Pro Se Press, and is currently writing his fourth adventure of New Orleans based private detective/jazz sdeman "Red" Gammon and his supernatural femme fatale associate.

BARON, MIKE
Born—7 Jan 1949
Fort Collins, CO

website: www.bloodyredbaron.com
E-mail: (baron.m@comcast.net)
Writer. @BloodyRedBaron on Twitter.
Mike Baron is a prolific comic book writer and novelist, best known for creating the science fiction comic Nexus, with illustrator Steve Rude, and the crazy costumed hero Badger. He has written Punisher, Star Wars, Flash, Deadman, and many other titles. He has won two Eisners. Ten years ago he began writing novels. There are seven Josh Pratt Biker novels. He has written three horror novels, Banshees, Skorpio, and Domain. He is the author of Florida Man, a novel about the trials of a struggling roofer in the Sunshine State.

BARROWS, BRANDON
Located in New England
website: www.brandonbarrowscomics.com
Twitter - @BrandonBarrows

Writer

Brandon Barrows primarily writes crime, mystery, and western stories. He is the author of the occult-noir novel *This Rough Old World* and the hard-boiled crime novel *Burn Me Out* as well as over fifty published stories, selected of which have been collected into the books *The Altar in the Hills* and *The Castle-Town Tragedy*. Brandon Barrows is also the writer of nearly one-hundred individual comic book issues. His comic work includes *Jack Hammer* from Action Lab Comics, which pays homage to both crime noir and the world of superheroes, and *Mythos* from Caliber Comics, based in the worlds of Lovecraftian horror, as well as a many other series and stories. He is an active member of the Private Eye Writers of America.

BASTIANELLI, GREGORY
Born—23 Oct 1959
Dover, NH
United States of America
Dover, NH

Website—www.gregprubastianelli.com

Twitter - @gregorybastiane
Instagram—gregorybastianelli.author
E-mail:(gregorybastianelli@yahoo.com)

Writer

Horror and pulp writer. Author of the horror novels "Jokers Club," "Loonies," and "Snowball." Author of the pulp novellas "The Dungeon of Death," in "Dan Fowler—G-Man, Volume One" and "The Lair of the Mole People," in "Men and Women of Mystery, Vol. Two." Author of several short stories appearing in multiple genre publications. Is a member of the Horror Writers Association and the New England Horror Writers. Second place award winner in the JournalStone Horror Novel Contest in 2011 for "Jokers Club."

BEALE, PAUL
Born—9 Nov 1962
560 Havelock Street
Saint John, N.B
Canada
E2M 2Y2

E-mail: (sjpigeons@gmail.com)

Writer—Artist—Editor
Comic book writer and editor, pulps/ short story writer and is well known as the writer, editor and sometimes artist of four comics for "Red Leaf Comics"—" All Canadian", "All Christian", "All Action Hero" and "All Western." He has also contributed several scripts for comics edited by friend Jim Hachey including "The Supernatural Agents" and "Manga Ganda." Paul has also done freelance writing for other publishers such as "Pilot Studios." Paul's biggest break in comics came when "Antartic Press" accepted his "Hidden Island" story for "Jungle Comics #3." That comic has been delayed by the Corona Virus but should be out later in 2020. Paul's non comic book work includes short stories for online magazine "Sci—fi Max" such as "The Waves" and "Gemstone." He received another big break when Airship 27 accepted his "Three Musketeers: Lady of Acadia" which will soon be published in "The Musketeers the New Adventures volume 1."

BEATTIE, BRYCE
Born—July 1979
3187 S. Hwy 89
Bountiful, UT 84010
United States of America

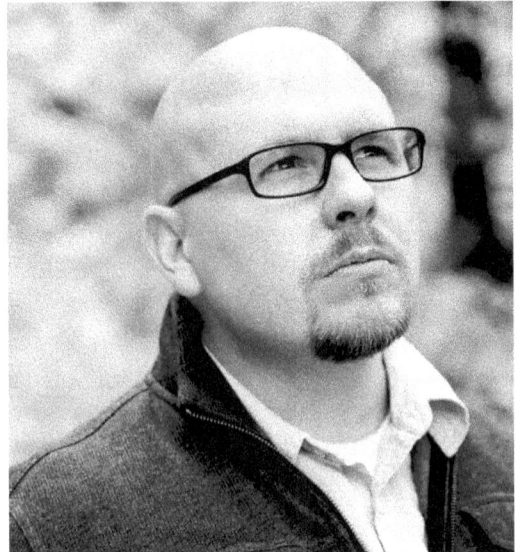

website: storyhack.com
E-mail: (bryce@storyhack.com)

Writer—Editor—Publisher

Bryce edits and publishes the modern pulp short fiction magazine StoryHack Action &

Adventure. When he's not busy dreaming up better ways to promote the magazine, he writes his own lively tales of derring-do which have earned spots in such venerable magazines as Astonishing Adventures Magazine, Occult Detective Magazine, and Weirdbook. When he's not working with fiction, he's programming web apps and managing the IT needs of a haunted hotel. He loves jazz and blues music, firearms, pulp magazines, programming, computer security topics, escape rooms, brisket & other smoked meats, high fives, kettlebells, two-wheeled transportation, his wife, and his kids. Not exactly in that order, though.

BELL, CHRIS
Born—12 Sep 1962
3333 N. Marshfield Ave.
Chicago, IL 60657
United States of America

website: chicagobagman.blogspot.com
E-mail: (Pulpscribe@gmail.com)

Writer - Reviewer

B. C. Bell is best known as the creator and writer of the Tales of The Bagman series. *("...be there, or miss out on the invention of the greatest new American pulp imagination at work in decades!!!!"—Keith Allan Deutsch, Publisher Black Mask Magazine)* Besides his sci-fi/horror novel Bipolar Express, Bell has authored over a dozen published pulp novellas featuring characters ranging from The Avenger to Secret Agent X. He also writes the Tales of The Bagman Blog where he searches for the rare, reviews books and magazines, philosophizes on writing, history, pop culture and the lack of a modern day pocket-size paperback.

BENNETT, ADAM
Born—14 Sept 1988
Fort St. John, BC
Canada

Facebook - @adambennettpulps
E-mail: (adamtbennett@gmail.com)

Writer—Artist—Publisher

Comic books and pulps writer here with the goal of create exciting stories and worlds to escape to. Escapism is the word, my love of comic books as a youth turned into wanting to become a writer, starting with short stories then moving into writing comic books as an adult. Currently I self publish a book series called Adam T Bennett Pulps, filled with novellas and short stories. Some based off of comic book scripts I wrote in the past and characters I created as a teenager. Self publishing my work I get to enjoy writing exactly

Art by Guy Davis

Art by Rob Davis

the way I want to and what I want to at any given time. The freedom to create is what I love, from superhero stories to western/ horror shorts. Taking what I've learned about storytelling from comics has been an asset for my series pacing, action and dialogue. So sit back and enjoy the current pulps with the spirit of the old and let the stories take you away for moment or two.

BENSON, RAYMOND
Born—6 Sep 1955

website: www.raymondbenson.com
E-mail: (admin@raymondbenson.com)

Writer—Musician/Composer—Film Historian/Instructor

Author of 40+ books, Raymond is best known for being the third—and first American—writer to be commissioned by the James Bond literary copyright holders to pen continuation 007 novels between 1996-2002. In total he wrote six original Bond novels, three movie novelizations, and three short stories—all published worldwide. His book THE JAMES BOND BEDSIDE COMPANION, first published in 1984, was nominated for an Edgar Allan Poe Award by Mystery Writers of America for Best Biographical/Critical Work. The critically acclaimed and award-winning serial thrillers, THE BLACK STILETTO, THE BLACK STILETTO: BLACK & WHITE, THE BLACK STILETTO: STARS & STRIPES, THE BLACK STILETTO: SECRETS & LIES, and THE BLACK STILETTO: ENDINGS & BEGINNINGS, were published between 2011 and 2014. The e-book anthology, THE BLACK STILETTO—THE COMPLETE SAGA, has been a continual best-seller. His most recent suspense novels include HOTEL DESTINY—A GHOST NOIR, BLUES IN THE DARK, IN THE HUSH OF THE NIGHT, and THE SECRETS ON CHICORY LANE. Other original thrillers include SWEETIE'S DIAMONDS, A HARD DAY'S DEATH, and DARK SIDE OF THE MORGUE (the latter nominated for the "Shamus Award" by the Private Eye Writers of America). Among Raymond's many media tie-in books are TOM CLANCY'S SPLINTER CELL and its sequel, TOM CLANCY'S SPLINTER CELL—OPERATION BARRACUDA (both written under the pseudonym "David Michaels"), which were *NY Times* Best-Sellers in 2004 and 2005. Raymond also spent over a decade in New York City, directing numerous stage productions and composing music for many shows. He recently won "Best Original Score" from the Vegas Movie Awards for his piano score for the short film, *Ghosts in the Ink* (2019), and he is previously the recipient of ten ASCAP Popular Music Awards.

BEZECNY, ATOM MUDMAN
Born—16 Aug 1994

website: www.oddtalesofwonder.com

E-mail: (oddtalesofwonder@gmail.com)
Writer—Editor—Publisher

Pulp writer and editor is the author of the books Tail of the Lizard King, Deus Mega Therion, Kinyonga Tales, Jim Anthony vs. the Mastermind, Meta-Terrax, Quinary Infinities, Gatherings, The New Adventures of Flash Avenger, and The Brute! A Speculative Study of Tarzan in Film. Her online publications include Dieselworld, Words from the Inner Circle, and The Monogram Monograph, and her short stories have appeared in anthologies from Airship 27 Productions, Pro Se Productions, and Black Coat Press. She is the editor-in-chief of Odd Tales Productions, a New Pulp publisher, and managed its ten-issue magazine Odd Tales of Wonder. She is the creator of the pulp hero Bloody Mary and has written stories of many classic characters from pulp fiction, including Ki-Gor, Jim Anthony, the Domino Lady, Harry Dickson, Doctor Omega, and others.

BIENIEK, MATTHEW
Brookfield, IL
United States of America

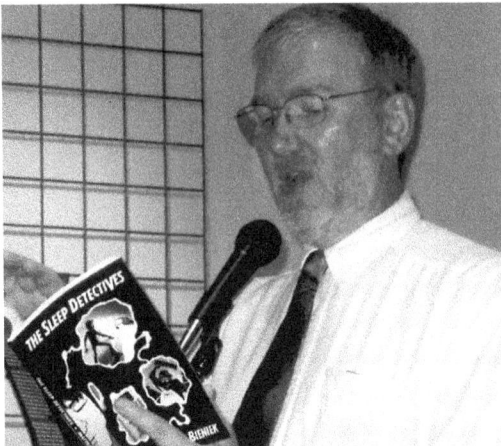

website: http://www.storiesbymatt.net/
E-mail: (matthew.bieniek@gmail.com)

Writer

Self-published writer, best known for his work on the Sleep Detectives series, as well as the Barnstormers trilogy, and stories featuring the customers and crew of a fictional comic shop called the Adventure Comics Comics Emporium. He is a regular open mic reader at the popular Tamale Hut Café Reading Series in North Riverside, IL, and is the founder and coordinator of the Tamale Hut Café Writers Group since 2013. Matt works as an IT professional by day, and has been a pulp fan since his parents bought him a paperback copy of the first Avenger novel, Justice, Inc., in the mid '70s.

BIRGE, KEVIN
Born—10 Nov 1966
408 Longview West
Moberly, MO 65270
United States of American
E-mail: (birge.kevin@gmail.com

Writer—Scripter—Reviewer

Staff writer for TSR Multiverse, where he supplies reviews, articles, and fiction. Has one work in print, in the first issue of The Crow Literary Journal. Currently researching material for an upcoming Professor Challenger tale for Airship 27.

BISHOP, PAUL
Born—April 1954
North of Los Angeles
California, USA

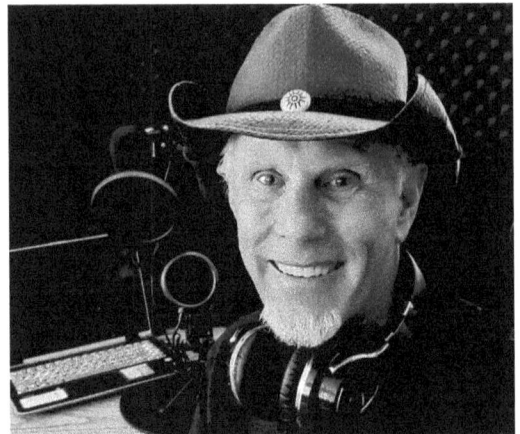

website: www.paulbishopbooks.com/

website: www.sixgunjustice.com/
E-mail:: bishsbeat@gmail.com/

Writer—Editor—Publisher—Podcaster

Novelist, screenwriter, and television personality, Paul Bishop is a nationally recognized interrogator and behaviorist. His thirty-five year career with the Los Angeles Police Department included three years with the department's Anti-Terrorist Division and over twenty years investigating sexual assaults. Twice selected as LAPD's Detective of the Year, his high profile Special Assault Units regularly produced the highest number of detective initiated arrests and crime clearance rates in the city. The author of fifteen novels (including the award winning Lie Catchers and five books in his LAPD Homicide Detective Fey Croaker series), Paul has written for episodic television and feature films, and also starred as the lead interrogator on the ABC TV reality show Take the Money and Run. As an enthusiast of the Western genre, he co-hosts the popular Six-Gun Justice Podcast and is the author of three highly regarded Western reference book, 52 Weeks—52 Western Novels, 52 Weeks—52 Western Movies, and 52 Weeks—52 Western TV Shows. Along with conducting law enforcement related seminars and continuing to consult on both criminal and civil investigations, he is currently the acquisition editor for Wolfpack Publishing.

BLACK, MICHAEL
Chicago, Il.
United States of America

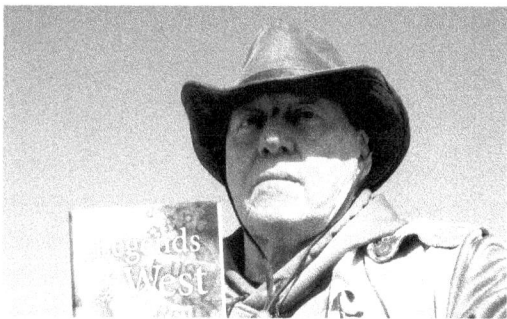

Writer

Michael A. Black is the award winning author of 40 books, most of which are in the mystery and thriller genres. He has also written in the sci-fi, western, horror, and sports genres. A former U.S. Army Military Policeman and retired Police Officer, he has done everything from patrol to investigating homicides to conducting numerous SWAT operations. Black was awarded the Cook County Medal of Merit in 2010. He is also the author of over 100 short stories and articles, and wrote two novels with television star, Richard Belzer (*Law & Order SVU*). Black is currently writing the Executioner series under the name Don Pendleton. His Executioner novel, *Fatal Prescription*, won the Best Original Novel Scribe Award given by the International Association of Media Tie-In Writers in 2018. A lifelong fan of the pulps, he writes the Doc Atlas series with his friend, Ray Lovato. Black's latest novels are *Trackdown: Devil's Dance* and *Legends of the West* (under his own name), *Dying Art* and *Cold Fury* (under Don Pendleton), and *Gunslinger: Killer's Choice/* Gunslinger: Killer's Ghost (under the name A.W. Hart).

BLALOCK, H DAVID
Born—16 September 1953
PO Box 307
Moscow, Tennessee 38057
United States of America

website: http://www.thrankeep.com
E-mail: (hdavidblalock@gmail.com)

Writer—Editor—Reviewer

H. David Blalock has been writing speculative fiction for nearly 50 years. His work has appeared in novels, novellas, stories, articles, anthologies, reviews, and commentary both in print and online. Since 1996, his fiction has appeared in over two dozen magazines including *Pro Se Presents*, *Alternate Realities*, *Alternate Species Magazine*,

Aphelion Webzine, Quantum Muse, Shelter of Daylight Magazine, The Harrow, The Three-Lobed Burning Eye, The Fifth Di…,The Martian Wave and many more. Anthologies featuring his work include *The Big Bad, The New Adventures of Foster Fade, Dreams of Steam, Southern Haunts*, and many others. His current novel series is the three book Angelkiller Triad from Seventh Star Press. He has edited several anthologies, including *NovoPulp, Idolaters of Cthulhu, Miskatonic Dreams, The Mad Visions of Al-Hazred*, and *City in the Ice*. He is currently the lead editor of *parABnormal Magazine* from Hiraeth Publishing. His work continues to appear on a regular basis through multiple publishing houses.

BLAYLOCK, JR., SIDNEY

Born - 16 Feb 1973
2107 Robbins St.
Chattanooga, TN 37404

website - http://sidneyblaylockjr.word-press.com
E-mail: (scblaylockjr@gmail.com)

Writer

Science Fiction and Fantasy writer, and PhD student. Best known for his short stories, many infused with new pulp sensibilities, he also writes in the comics/graphic novels genre, creating and writing "The Scream-Team" for the indie Cynosure Comics in the late 90s. His story "Faerie Knight," published in the anthology, *Fae*, and edited by Rhonda Parrish, was a Starred Review for the Tangent Online Recommended Reading List for 2014. His most recent short-story, "HawkeMoon" was selected as the cover story for the new pulp magazine, *Storyhack Action and Adventure*, Issue 4, edited by Bryce Beattie. Other publications include electricspec.com, *Tales of the Talisman*, and the *Visions* series of anthologies (*Visions IV: The Space Between Stars* and *Visions VI: Galaxies*).

BONADONNA, JOE

Born—January 25, 1952
Chicago, IL
Amazon Author's page at: www.amazon.com/Joe-Bonadonna/e/B009I1KYIK
His Facebook page is called Bonadonna's Bookshelf, at: https://www.facebook.com/BonadonnasBookshelf/

Writer — Reviewer

Author of the heroic fantasies *Mad Shadows-Book One: The Weird Tales of Dorgo the Dowser* (winner of the 2017 Golden Book Readers' Choice Award for Fantasy); *Mad Shadows-Book 2: Dorgo the Dowser and the Order of the Serpent*; the space opera *Three Against The Stars*; the sword and planet space adventure, *The MechMen of Canis-9*; and the sword & sorcery adventure, *Waters of Darkness*, in collaboration with David C. Smith. With co-writer Erika M Szabo, he wrote *Three Ghosts in a Black Pumpkin* (winner of the 2017 Golden Books Judge's Choice Award for Children's Fantasy), and *The Power of the Sapphire Wand*. He also has stories appearing in: *Azieran—Artifacts and Relics, GRIOTS 2: Sisters of the Spear, Heroika: Dragon Eaters, Poets in Hell, Doctors in Hell, Pirates in Hell, Lovers in Hell, Mystics in Hell*; and *Sinbad: The New Voyages, Volume 4*. With author Shebat Legion, he co-wrote *Samuel Meant Well and the Little Black Cloud of the Apocalypse*, for the shared-world anthology *Sha'Daa Toys*; and with David C. Smith he co-wrote *To Save Hermesia*, for the sword and planet anthology *The Lost Empire of Sol*. In addition to his fiction, he has written a number of articles, book, and movie reviews for Black Gate online magazine.

BOOP, DAVID

Born—23 JULY 1968
Denver, CO 80237
United States of America

website: www.davidboop.com
E-mail: DAVID@DAVIDBOOP.COM

Writer—Editor—Publisher

Boop's first novel, "She Murdered Me with Science" (WordFire Press, 2016), is a pulpy blend of science fiction and noir. He self-published a prequel, "A Whisper to a Scheme," through his company, Longshot Productions. Boop has written for several prominent pulp characters including *The Green Hornet, Flash Gordon, The Black Bat,* and *Domino Lady*, plus created his own pulp characters like the leatherhead football-era vigilante, *Gridiron*. Additionally, Boop has worked with other licensed properties such as *The Rippers* RPG (Pinnacle Entertainment Group), *Predator* (Titan Publishing), and *Veronica Mars* (Amazon). He has written and/or produced short films, some which can be seen on Longshot Productions' YouTube Channel. His short fiction work covers a wide range of genres, including the interconnected weird western series, "The Drowned Horse Chronicle," and the quarterly flash-fiction mystery series, "The Trace Walker Temporary Mysteries," (appearing on Gumshoereview.com). As an anthologist, Boop has edited the weird western *Straight Outta* series (Baen Books), a forthcoming space western anthology series (also Baen Books), and the *Domino Lady* anthology, "Gentlemen Prefer Domino Lady" (Moonstone Books). He does developmental editing for other publishers or mentors students and authors in his "copious" free time. His current obsessions include anime, *The Nightmare Before Christmas*, and Funko Pops. He has a son, doesn't sleep, and can be usually found on Facebook or Twiter.

BOUSQUET, MARK
Born—30 March 1973
Scranton, PA 18505
United States of America

website: themarkbousquet.com
E-mail: (bousquet.mark@gmail.com)

Writer—Editor—Publisher

Primarily working as a writer, he is best known for his Gunfighter Gothic (weird western) and Spooky Lemon (mystery) series. In total, he has published over a dozen novels in a wide variety of genres: Used the Be: The Kid Rapscallion Story (superhero), The Haunting of Kraken Moor (horror), American Hercules (action), Harpsichord & The Wormhole Witches (science fiction), and Dreamer's Syndrome (modern fantasy). Though mostly self-publishing through his own Space Buggy Press imprint, he has produced stories for a range of publishers, including New Pulp projects for White Rocket Books, Pro Se Press,

Airship 27, and PulpWork Press. He has also published a range of adventure fiction for kids, including Adventures of the Five, Stuffed Animals for Hire, and The Bear at the Top of the Stairs.

BRODEN, KEVIN PAUL SHAW
Born—11 June 1967
PO Box 6385
Burbank, CA 91510
United States of America

E-mail:friendsofmaskedghost@gmail.com

Writer - Artist

Kevin got his start as an artist assistant at Image Comics, seguing over into New Pulp with his art and writing skills. He's best known for his MASKED GHOST stories, with his book REVENGE OF THE MASKED GHOST appearing on Derrick Ferguson's list of New Pulp Books To Get You Started. His work appears as the cover art for NEWSHOUDS by Pro Se Press, and he has also done interior illustrations for several books for Airship 27 Productions. You can find his work in THE BAY PHANTOM: FEAST OF THE CANNIBAL GUILD by Chuck Miller (nominated for Best Novel in the 2019 Pulp Factory Awards), THE PERSONA: GREEN FLESHED FIENDS by Michael Housel, and the short story by Ralph L. Angelo Jr. in LEGENDS OF NEW PULP FICTION (Best Anthology Winner for Pulp Factory Awards 2015). In New Pulp comics, Kevin both wrote and illustrated the story "The

D.A.'s Dilemma" featuring the Veiled Avenger in ALL-STAR PULP COMICS #4 for Redbud Studios and Airship 27. Additionally, his stories have appeared in the anthologies NEWSHOUNDS ("Stop the Presses!") and BLACK FEDORA ("The Man Who Stole Manhattan"), the latter of which was a nominee for Best Collection/Anthology for New Pulp Awards 2014. Husband of New Pulp Writer Shannon Muir.

BROWN, MICHAEL
Born—8 Sept 1964
Tamarac, FL 33321
United States of America

website: the pulp.net/pulpsuperfan/
E-mail: (emb021@yahoo.com

Reviewer

Reviewer and amateur researcher best known for his blog at ThePulp.net under the heading of The Pulp Super-fan. Over 600 posting have been done since March of 2013. While the main focus has been on original pulp, the blog has also included reviews of pulp-related comics and movies, looked at foreign pulp as well as some of the fore-runners of pulp. Pulp successors like techno-thrillers and New Pulp are also covered. Postings on publishers, references and fanzines are also included. The postings try to go beyond just being basic reviews of the work to give information on the characters and authors to help the reader better appreciate the works and the history of the Pulps.

BRYANT, STEVE
Born—August 26, Generation X
Between Chicago and St. Louis
United States of America

website: SteveBryantComics.com
E-mail: (SteveBryantArt@gmail.com)

Artist - Writer - Raconteur

Steve Bryant is the Eisner, Manning, and Harvey Award-nominated creator/writer/artist of the pulp comic series **Athena Voltaire** from Action Lab Entertainment, and the writer/co-creator of **Ghoul Scouts**, an all-ages adventure comic also published by Action Lab. Other comic projects include **The Catch** (writer/co-creator/variant cover artist), the webcomic **Maximus Wrecks** (creator/writer/artist), a tie-in to the Fox Television series 24 (artist), and an adaptation of Oscar Wilde's **The Canterville Ghost** (artist).

He has also completed projects for Dark Horse Comics, Image Comics, IDW, Boom! Studios, Ape Entertainment, Moonstone Books, and others, as well as extensive work in the roleplaying and boardgame industry. When he's not making comics, Bryant is an Assistant Professor in the Creative Technologies department at Illinois State University, teaching Digital Painting. He lives in the suburban wilds of Central Illinois with his family and companion animals.

BULLOCK, MIKE
Born—15 Sept 1970
South Texas
United States of America

website: https://www.facebook.com/RunemasterPress/
E-mail: (mike@runemasterstudios.com)

Writer—Editor

Comics and pulps writer/editor best known as the creator of the all-ages comic series *Lions, Tigers and Bears*, Bullock also holds the distinction of penning more comic book stories of Lee Falk's Phantom than any other writer in American history. Bullock assumed the role of Phantom Group Editor, overseeing Moonstone's entire Phantom line in the final years of their original run with the character. Pulp works include a re-imagined Black Bat for Moonstone Books, as well as Air Boy, Gladiator, Captain Future, Golden Amazon and more. Co-architect of the Moonstone Books *Return of the Originals* pulp universe, Bullock is also the creator of original New Pulp characters Death Angel, Dr. Dusk, Dynamo Jack, The Runemaster and Xander Janus: Guardian of Worlds.

BURNETT, MISHA
Born—9 Aug 1963
St. Louis, MO 63117

Art by James Lyle

website: https://mishaburnett.wordpress.com/
E-mail: (mjb63114@gmail.com)

Writer

Although he is the author of *The Book Of Lost Doors* series of novels, Misha Burnett is primarily a short story writer. His story "In The City Of Dreadful Joy" was the third place finalist in the 2019 Baen Fantasy Short Fiction Contest. Collections include *Duel Visions*, with author Louise Sorensen, published by Cirsova Publishing and *Bad Dreams & Broken Hearts: The Case Files Of Erik Rugar*, published by Lagrange Books. A third collection, *Dark Fantasies*, is scheduled for summer of 2020, from Storyhack Press.

His stories have appeared in Switchblade Magazine, Tuscany Bay Books Planetary Anthologies, Millhaven Tales, and numerous independently published anthologies.

CAREY, WAYNE
Born—8 Jun 1955
1267 West Loop Road
Hollidaysburg, PA 16648
United States of America

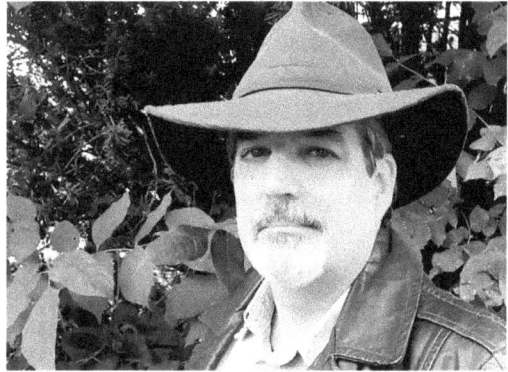

website: www.wgcarey.com
E-mail: (wgcarey@ProtonMail.com)

Writer

A former pharmaceutical research scientist, he is the author of The Nanon Factor (Leo Publishing, 2015), a contemporary science fiction thriller involving nanotechnology. He has contributed two novels to the expanded Allan Quatermain canon, H. Rider Haggard's classic hero, from Airship 27 Productions' Quatermain: The New Adventures, including Allan Quatermain and the Beast Men (2018) and Allan Quatermain and the Lightning Bird (2018). Airship 27 has also released Company of Shadows (2019), his novel of modern day Civil War reenactors caught in a supernatural battle. His short fiction has appeared in numerous anthologies, including the award winning Legends of New Pulp Fiction (Airship 27 2015) and The Clan Chronicles: Tales from Plexis, edited by Julie E. Czerneda (DAW 2018).

CASEY, JONATHAN
Born—1991
Warrior Run, PA
United States of America
Youtube Channel: https://www.youtube.com/channel/UCdq_GQ1uyW7B-UAIrnrezjg?view_as=subscriber
E-mail: (taylor67914@yahoo.com)

Writer

Short story writer whose first published

story was "The Adventure of the Irregular Heartbeat" in Sherlock Holmes: Consulting Detective Volume 15 by Airship 27 Productions. He is currently in the process of writing an adventure story featuring Professor George Edward Challenger. He has also written many as-yet unpublished short stories for many years. He is an avid guitar player/singer-songwriter. He is a Child Welfare Caseworker who majored in the field of Criminology at Wilkes University.

CATTO, ED

Born—5 June 1963
304 N. Hoopes Avenue
Auburn, NY 13021 United States of America

website www.agendaegroup.com

Artist—Writer—Educator - Columnist

Comics and pulp illustrator/writer is known for his illustrations in Airship 27 Adventures of Captain Graves, Company of Shadows, Ravenwood Stepson of Mystery (Vol. 3) and Crazy 8's Zlonk, Zok, Zowie. Catto's comics work has appeared in AHOY, Dynamite, American Mythology and Moonstone comics. At Captain Action Enterprises, Catto manages the Captain Action brand. Catto recently served as Co-Editor for Clover Press' Pirates GN. A longtime convention enthusiast, Catto

helped develop and grow New York Comic Con and currently teaches a course on comic conventions at Ithaca College.

CHAMBERS, PEGGY

Born—10 Feb 1953 2801 Constitution Ave. Enid, OK 73703 United States of America

website: http://peggylchambers.com
E-mail: peggy.chambers@hotmail.com

Writer

Peggy Chambers is an award winning, multi-genre author. She writes a weekly blog at http://peggylchambers.com. Her books include the pulp fiction novel *The Apocalypse Sucks* (Airship 27), the *Glome's Valley* YA fantasy series (self-pub), the *Sandhill Island* suspense series (The Wild Rose Press), *Blooming Justice, The Keystone Lake Series* (suspense from The Wild Rose Press). Her novella, *Witches' Cliff,* (fantasy from The Wild Rose Press) was a finalist in the International Digital Awards through the Oklahoma Romance Writers of America and she has won numerous awards for short stories from Oklahoma Writers' Federation Inc. She's won awards for her writing at the Necatunga Arts Festival. Her story *Werewolves in the Park* found its way into Airship 27's *Legends of*

New Pulp Fiction. She is waiting on the debut of *Stone of Thor* her first comic script with Okie Comics and her novel *Flatiron Death Grip* is currently on the desk for publication with Airship 27.

CHINN, MIKE
Born—31 Dec 1954
137 Priory Road
Hall Green
Birmingham B28 0TG
United Kingdom

website: http://saladoth.blogspot.com
E-mail: (saladoth@hotmail.co.uk)

Writer—Editor

Scripted fourteen issues of the *Starblazer* digest comic book for DC Thompson between 1982-90; including five sword and sorcery tales concerning the d'Annemarc dynasty of Anglerre, and three slapstick SF adventures of the Robot Kid. Edited *Swords Against the Millennium* for The Alchemy Press in 2000, and three volumes of *The Alchemy Press Book of Pulp Heroes* (2012-14). Six of his Damian Paladin occult adventure stories were collected into *The Paladin Mandates* in 1998 and published by The Alchemy Press. The book was short-listed in the British Fantasy Awards in the Best

Collection and Best Short Story categories. In 2017 Pro Se Productions published a second volume of Paladin fiction, *Walkers in Shadow*.

COLE, ADRIAN
22nd July 1949
Bideford, Devon, UK
E-mail: (acole@btinternet.com)

Writer- Editor- Reviewer

Born in Plymouth, Devonshire, UK (Solomon Kane country) in 1949. His first published work was a pulp sword-&-planet trilogy, THE DREAM LORDS (Zebra, New York 1975/76) heavily influenced by ERB, DUNE and Wheatley! These appeared during the REH boom, with the legend "Heroic fantasy in the tradition of REH" emblazoned on the covers. Cole has written many novels and short stories, including The Omaran Saga (Avon US) described by reviewer Morgan Holmes as "...like Weird Tales written by Tolkien..." and the Voidal Saga, in which the Moorcock-like hero battles the gods of Darkness. The entire saga is available in 3 volumes from Wildside Press (US). Black Gate have fully reviewed it on their website, commenting "...this is technicolor, Cinemascope craziness..." Recently Cole has returned to writing new pulp, notably the Nick Nightmare stories, about a hard-boiled supernatural private eye, in Mickey

Spillane vein—the self-styled Private Eye, Public Fist battles every kind of monster, from Cthulhu Mythos aberrations to black magic, demonology and anything the legions of Hell can spawn. NICK NIGHTMARE INVESTIGATES, the first collected volume, won the prestigious British Fantasy Award for Best Collection of 2015. NIGHTMARE COCKTAILS and NIGHTMARE CREATURES (Pulp Hero Press, US) are due later this year. Strongly influenced by REH's S&S yarns, Cole has also written new Elak of Atlantis stories, utilizing Henry Kuttner's celebrated character. ELAK, KING OF ATLANTIS is due from Pulp Hero Press soon, collecting the first batch. Also due are DARK SHIPS PASSING, a collection of Cole's S&S tales (including new material), A DEATH IN PULPWORLD and reprints of the DREAM LORDS. Cole has also written many other Cthulhu Mythos stories and is a regular contributor to magazines such as Cirsova, Weirdbook, Heroic Fantasy Quarterly and Tales from the Magician's Skull. He has been translated into several foreign languages.

COLLINS, MAX ALLAN
Born—3 Mar 1948
301 Fairview Avenue
Muscatine, IA 52761
United States of America

website: www.maxallancollins.com

E-mail: (maphilms@hotmail.com)

Writer—Screenwriter—Editor—Musician

Collins is best known for writing the graphic novel *Road to Perdition*, basis of the Academy Award-winning 2002 film starring Tom Hanks, and the Nathan Heller and Quarry mystery series. Heller is a classic private detective involved in famous real-life crimes of the 20th Century; Quarry is the first hitman in mystery fiction to helm a series. He is a Mystery Writers of America Grand Master, has won Shamus and Anthony awards, and is recipient of the Private Eye Writers of America Grand Master, the Eye. He began publishing in 1973 with *Bait Money*, first novel in the Nolan series, and entered the comics field taking over the writing of *Dick Tracy* from creator Chester Gould, scripting it from 1977 through 1993. As an independent filmmaker in his native Iowa, he has directed two documentaries and four features, including the Lifetime film *Mommy,* and written several others; the Quarry novels became a Cinemax TV series in 2016. He created the long-running *Ms. Tree* comics feature with artist Terry Beatty and has written *Batman* and another Collins/Beatty creation, *Wild Dog*. He often writes with his wife Barbara, notably the *Antiques* cozy mystery series (as "Barbara Allan"). His friendship with Mickey Spillane led to Collins completing numerous novels and stories in the legendary mystery writer's files, including the Mike Hammer series. His non-fiction works include *The History of Mystery, Scarface and the Untouchable* and *Eliot Ness and the Mad Butcher* (the latter two with A. Brad Schwartz). His other mystery series include Mallory, Jack and Maggie Starr, and Reeder and Rogers (with Matthew Clemens), and he has written numerous bestselling TV and movie movie tie-in novels, including *Saving Private Ryan* and *American Gangster*. (Photo—John Deason)

CONSTANTINE, PERCIVAL
Born—12 Aug 1983
Kagoshima City
Kagoshima Prefecture
Japan

website: percivalconstantine.com
E-mail:pc@percivalconstantine.com

Writer—Editor—Publisher—Artist

Born and raised in Chicago, Percival Constantine is a prolific creator who has written dozens of novels and has contributed to a number of prose and comic book anthologies for publishers such as Pro Se Press, Airship 27, Moonstone Books, and PulpWork Press. His work has spanned a number of genres including urban fantasy, superhero, science fiction, mystery, horror, and action/adventure. Among his most-popular series are The Myth Hunter (pulp adventure), Vanguard (superhero), and the best-selling Luther Cross (urban fantasy). He also hosts the Superhero Cinephiles podcast with fellow New Pulp author Derrick Ferguson and the Japan On Film podcast. He resides in southern Japan where he teaches college classes in film, literature, and EFL while continuing to produce books and comics.

COOPER, ART
3520 Loyalist Drive
Mississauga, ON
Canada L5L 4W5
E-mail: art.1957@gmail.com

Artist—Writer—Editor

Art is a Canadian artist/writer/editor who was a founding partner of Spectrum Publications, which published three bimonthly mini-comics in the early 1970s. In 1972 he was a member of the inaugural Cartooning program at Sheridan College in Oakville, Ontario, where the guest instructors included such luminaries as Joe Kubert, Neal Adams, Bernie Wrightson

and Will Eisner. Art contributed to a number of small press publications and penciled two stories for Orb Magazine. Since 2015, Art has provided Ron Fortier's **Airship 27 Productions** with interior illustrations for six New Pulp books, including Mark Justice's Dead Sheriff 1 & 2.

COWAN, JD

website: wastelandadsky.blogspot.ca
E-mail: (lonewolfandJD@gmail.com)

Writer

JD Cowan is a writer of short stories, novellas, novelettes, and novels. He has contributed to StoryHack magazine, the PulpRev Sampler, and the free "Corona-Chan: Spreading the Love" anthology, among many others. His books have both been independently published and through presses such as Silver Empire. Cowan writes action stories and weird tales with a moral and superversive sensibility. His stories range from the portal adventure of the "Gemini Man" series to the noir bent of "Someone is Aiming for You & Other Adventures" and "Grey Cat Blues". He talks about entertainment and art at his blog Wasteland & Sky.

COZORT, DALE
Dekalb, IL 60115
United States of America

website: www.DaleCozort.com
E-mail: (DaleCoz2@gmail.com)

Writer - Reviewer

New Pulp and Science Fiction writer is best known for his numerous Snapshot novels and novellas, including Jace of the Jungle, a modern take on the Jungle Adventure story and The Necklace of Time, a novel where the modern US meets a mutated version of the US 1950s in a strange universe with an endless frontier. His short stories Fire and the Blood of Innocents and A Dad Should Have Nightmares appeared in Legends of New Pulp anthology and the Alternate Peace anthology respectively.

CRAM, JEFF
Born—1 Feb 1977
217 Center St.
Old Town, ME 04468
United States of America

website – https://www.instagram.com/cramnation/
E-mail: (cramnation@gmail.com)

Artist

Graduate of the Joe Kubert Schoool of Cartoon and Graphic Art, Inc. Professional illustrator for over 15 years. Works include comic book art, as well as spot illustration for role-playing game publications, and inumerable private commissions. Clients include Chaos Comics, Herogames, Green Ronin Publishing, Mongoose Publishing. Currently illustrator for Airship 27 Productions, a leading New Pulp Fiction publisher.

CRAIG, BILLY
Born –21, Nov 1959
New Castle, Indiana
United States of America
E-mail: (pop_cat@hotmail.com)

Writer

Craig is best known for his Hardluck Hannigan series and his hard-boiled Key West Mystery series featuring Private Investigator Rick Marlow. Craig has published several best-selling mysteries as well as some science fiction and westerns.

CRAIG, BOBBY
Born—22 July 1966
8664 Chase Drive
Chagrin Falls, OH 44023
United States of America

website –pulpfarm.com
E-mail: (bcraig@pulpfarm.com)

Writer

Writer of the new pulp adventures of the Green Lama and the Moon Man for Airship 27 Productions. He is the lead marketing strategist and maker for the Pulp Farm, the parent company for his various advertising firms and consulting ventures. When he established the Pulp Farm, it was named in tribute to the pulp industry where creatives worked quickly and aimed for a visceral response. Always a fan of masked heroes, two-fisted detectives, and shudder pulps, Bobby considers himself fortunate to have studied pulp and detective fiction under the tutelage of award-winning pulp historians Garyn Roberts and Gary Hoppenstand at Bowling Green State University. Currently, he is planning for new adventures of the Domino Lady, the Green Ghost, as well as a multi-character, jungle pulp thriller.

CROWLEY, TERRY
Born 24 April, 1968
Po Box 272572 Fort Collins, CO 80527
United States of America

website - https://vimhoodchronicles.com
E-mail:terry.crowley1999@gmail.com

Writer - Reviewer

Terry Mark is a former Presidential campaign advisor and a Webmaster in the NHL. He has written restaurant and film reviews for magazine. He also has a 6 page comic strip in Front Range Tales #3 which is the precursor to his next series. He has completed the first two novels in his Vim Hood Chronicles trilogy: Kill The Night and And The Sun Goeth Down, and is working on the finale - Moonlight Serenade, which will be finished in 2021.

CRUZ, FELIX
Born—1977
Philadelphia, PA
United States of America

E-mail: (felixwritesstuff@gmail.com)

Writer—Editor

As a recent contributor to the New Pulp Fiction universe, Cruz has written several upcoming stories, including "The Purple Scar: The Scar's Close Shave" for Airship 27 Productions, and a Dr. John Silence story for Pro Se Productions. His previous short story "Father's Day" was published in *A Twist of Noir*. In addition, he has written crime novels, including *Rushing the Row* and *Daddy's Little Boys*. When Cruz is not writing, he works as a book editor. His edited works include Charles Carfagno, Jr.'s fantasy novel *A Demon's Quest: The Beginning of the End*, the first entry in the *A Demon's Quest* trilogy. Cruz is currently working on his latest crime novel and other stories for New Pulp Fiction publishers.

CRUZ, PEDRO
Born—24 Sep 1975
Portugal

website – www.pedro-cruz.blogspot.com
E-mail: (pedrocruzcomics@gmail.com)

Writer—Artist—Reviewer

An architect and teacher, he is also a comic book writer/artist and illustrator of pulps, having collaborated with illustrations and comics for numerous magazines and books. He won the portuguese Amadora BD Cartoon contest in 2002 and 2003. In the New Pulp movement, he has illustrated several books for leading publisher Airship 27 Productions, including "Jim Anthony: Super Detective", "The Amazing Harry Houdini" and "The Towers of Metropolis". He's the author of "The Mighty Enlil", nominated for best portuguese author comic book in a foreign language in 2014 at the comics International Festival of Amadora BD. He was part of the judging panel of the Comic-Con Portugal Comic Book Awards in 2018 and 2019. Recently, he made the art for "Mindex", a graphic novel published in 2020 by Kingpin Books. Currently, he writes and draws the webcomic "The Fine Game of Nil".

CUNNINGHAM, BILL
Born—27 February 1963
251 N. Brand Blvd. Suite 202 Glendale, CA 91203
United States of America

website: www.pulp2ohpress.com
E-mail:: cinexploits@gmail.com

Writer—Designer—Publisher   - Screenwriter - Producer

Pulp (re)designer and publisher is best known for over 25 pulp and comic collections published through his Pulp 2.0 label. Recent releases include the original graphic anthology *Tales of Frankenstein*, *The Mike Shayne Private Eye Comic Collection* restoring the 1962 Dell comic series, *Armageddon 2419 A.D.*, and Magazine Enterprises' *Strong Man* created by Bob Powell and Superman co-creator Jerry Siegel. He works fluidly between pulp, comics, and movies and is known for integrating each into his work. His writing has appeared in the first four volumes of the *Tales of the Shadowmen* series by Black Coat Press as well as several volumes of the pulp magazine *Astonishing Adventures*. His recent writing work is the successful *Cinexploits!* series of nonfiction film books - *Death Kiss: The Book of the Movie*, and *Automatons: The Book of the Movie*. He is rewriting and designing the legendary *Killer* Chilean comic book series, and translating the gothic *Terror*

Art by Kevin A. Johnson

Comics by Spain's renowned comic artist Joan Boix. His first professional work was creating "The Pixie" for DC Comics' Series *Dial H for Hero* in *Adventure Comics #488*. As a screenwriter-producer, he has written and/or conceived of many successful motion pictures including *Scarecrow* (with Jason White and Emmanuel Itier), *Scarecrow: Slayer*, *Dr. Chopper*, and others. He has also created and written Decoder Ring Theater's audio adventure *"The Murder Legion Strikes at Midnight,"* starring *The Knightmare*, an original pulp-style hero. His career has allowed him to create the marketing plans for over 100 films that have been sold worldwide. He received the writer award from the *2005 Variety Magazine DVD Premiere Awards*. He is currently developing several Pulp 2.0 properties into films and television and designing covers for the acclaimed magazines *Men of Violence, Pulp Horror, Monster Maniacs*, and *Hot Lead*.

DAVIS, GUY S.
Born—31 July 1972
Arvada Colorado
United States of America

website: gsdavisart.com
Facebook, Twitter, Instagram and

DeviantArt: GSDavisArt
E-mail: (guy@gsdavisart.com)

Artist

G.S.Davis is an artist hailing from the wilds of Arvada, Colorado. At the tender age of 15, he discovered that his calling was storytelling. Naturally he discovered this talent while trying to get out of trouble with his mother. As time went on, he evolved his talent and soon began writing comics. Now, many years later, he's still trying to avoid getting in trouble, though he believes that his wife is probably on to him at this point. Thus he tends to hide in his office, writing comics and putting them out into the world. He draws in two different styles: A cartoon style distantly reminiscent of the newspaper strips of yore, and a more serious Manga style, distantly reminiscent of Japanese comic books of yore.

DAVIS, MILTON
Fayetteville, GA
United States of America

website: miltonjdavis.com/

Writer—Editor Publisher

Milton Davis is an award winning Black Fantastic writer and owner of MVmedia, LLC, a publishing company specializing in Science Fiction, Fantasy and Sword and Soul. Milton is the author of twenty-three novels and editor/co-editor of seven anthologies. Milton's work had also been featured in *Black Power: The Superhero Anthology*; Skelos *2: The Journal of Weird Fiction and Dark Fantasy Volume 2*, *Steampunk Writes Around the World* published by Luna Press and *Bass Reeves Frontier Marshal Volume Two*. Milton's story 'The Swarm' was nominated for the 2018 British Science Fiction Association Award for Short Fiction. His screenplay, Ngolo, won the 2014 Urban Action Showcase Award for Best Screenplay.

DAVIS, ROB
Born -August 13, 1954
5200 E Mount Zion Church Road
Hallsville, MO 65255
United States of America

website: robmdavis.com
E-mail: (robmdavis@me.com)

Illustrator - Graphic Designer - Publisher

Comics and pulps artist and designer. Probably best known as the illustrator of Star Trek comics for DC and Malibu comics in the 1990s. He won the Pulp Factory Award for Best Pulp Interior Illustrations in 2009 and 2016 for illustrations in Sherlock Holmes Consulting Detective. He is the Art Director of Airship 27 Productions, a leading New Pulp Fiction publisher doing design work for all the books and illustrat-

ing many of them each year.

DECKER, DWIGHT R.
Born—26 Jan 1952
2902 King Arthur Ct.
Northlake, IL 60164
United States of America
E-mail: (deklane@aol.com)

Writer—Translator

Comics and science-fiction writer and translator best known for translating various episodes of the German PERRY RHODAN science-fiction adventure series. Has also worked as a translator of European-produced Disney comics from several languages into English. Currently working on his own projects, including translations of early German science fiction dating back to the 1700s, as well as original fantasy and science-fiction adventure, with several books available through Amazon. Reads old pulp science fiction, mostly from before 1950, and plans to write in that vein for as long as he is lucid.

DEIS, ROBERT
Born—28 Jan 1950
20913 Seventh Ave. West
Cudjoe Key, FL 33042

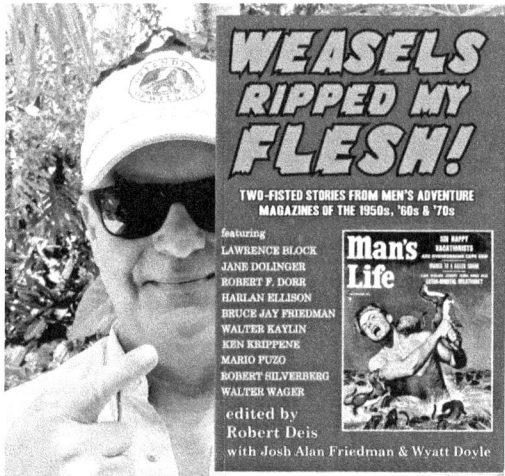

website: www.MensPulpMags.com

E-mail:cujokey@gmail.com

Writer—Editor—Publisher

Co-Editor, with Wyatt Doyle, of the Men's Adventure Library books series (published by New Texture), which features stories and artwork from vintage men's adventure magazines (MAMs) published in the 1950s, 1960s and 1970s. Maintains the MensPulpMags.com blog about MAMs and the Men's Adventure Magazines & Books Facebook Group. Bob's books include both illustrated story anthologies, such as *Weasels Ripped My Flesh!, He-Men, Bag Men & Nymphos, A Handful of Hell,* and *I Watched them Eat Me Alive,* as well as art books that focus on artists who did cover and interior illustrations for MAMs and action/adventure paperbacks, such as Mort Künstler, Samson Pollen and Gil Cohen, and notable artist's models they used, like Eva Lynd and Steve Holland.

DeVITO, JOE
Born—16 March 1957
115 Shady Hill Dr.
Chalfont, PA, 18914
United States of America

website: www.jdevito.com; www.kong-

skullisland.com
E-mail: (jdartworks@verizon.net)

Artist–Writer

Best known for painting, sculpting and writing about Pulp and Pop Culture icons—Illustrator and also co-authored with Brad Strickland of four novels: *KONG: King of Skull Island, Merian C. Cooper's KING KONG, King Kong of Skull Island: Exodus* and *King Kong of Skull Island: The Wall*—DeVito continues painting covers for Will Murray's *Wild Adventures* series, featuring Doc Savage, Pat Savage, Tarzan, The Shadow, The Spider, Operator 5, Sherlock Holmes, and King Kong—Creator of content, concept and character designs for the film, television, gaming, collectible and toy industries—Illustrated hundreds of book and magazine covers, posters and numerous trading cards for the major comic book and gaming houses—Paintings of others include King Kong, DC's Superman, Batman, Robin, Flash, Green Lantern and Wonder Woman, Supergirl, Catwoman; Marvel's Spider-man, Sandman, Dr. Octopus; and MAD magazine's Alfred E. Neuman—Sculptures include *Doc Savage* for Graphitti Design, the official 100th Anniversary statue of *Tarzan of the Apes* for the Edgar Rice Burroughs Estate, *The Cooper Kong* for the Merian C. Cooper Estate, Superman, Wonder Woman and Batman for DC Comics—Deeply rooted in the fine arts, Joe has sculpted monumental statues of the Madonna and Child, one of which is placed in Domus Pacis at the Our Lady of Fatima Shrine, in Portugal, bas-reliefs of St. Jude, and has restored the historic icon known as the Odessa Madonna, which now resides in Kazan, Russia—Founder of DeVito ArtWorks, LLC, an artist-driven transmedia studio dedicated to the creation and development of multi-faceted properties including *King Kong of Skull Island, War Eagles,* and the *Primordials.*

DILKS, STEVE Born—30 Nov 1971 Watford Hertfordshire United Kingdom

website – N/A
E-mail: (stevendilks@aol.com)

Writer—Editor—Publisher

As a writer he has been published in Weird Book, Startling Stories and Flashing Swords! His novellas of Gunthar, the Black Wolf of Tatukura, first began appearing as a series of e-books in 2013. Labeled as 'sword-&-sorcery' or 'sword-&-super science', they were collected together with a new story in the paperback, Gunthar-Warrior of the Lost World. A recent novella, Riders of the fire, is an addition to the post-nuke pulp genre. Under his own Carnelian Press imprint, he is the editor and publisher of two fanzines, The Hyborian Gazette and Twilight Echoes-Tales of swords & dark magic. The former is an appreciation to the continued legacy of Robert E. Howard while the latter publishes stories by new authors working in the field of heroic fantasy.

DIRSCHERL, FRANK
Born - 24 May 1973
PO Box 31
Wollongong NSW 2520
Australia

website - www.trinitycomics.com
E-mail: - admin@trinitycomics.com

Writer—Editor - Publisher

Frank Dirscherl is the author and editor of the Amazon bestselling books "Sanderson of Metro," "The Wraith" and "Beyond the Lens." His series of 'The Wraith Adventures' books have been enjoyed by multitudes of readers the world over. His latest, "Serpent Rising," is out now, with more to come in the future. A professionally certified library technician, who has been working in libraries for over twenty five years, Frank has also worked at a medical practice in a data entry position, covered books for a book wholesale company, as a lecturer to children on the merits, and writing, of comic books, and as an online activist for social equality. He lives on the south coast of New South Wales, Australia, with his beautiful wife Jennifer and their gorgeous daughter Emma, where he is currently working on his latest piece of fiction.

DIXON, CHUCK
Born—14 April 1954
Odessa, FL 33556
United States of America

DORAN, BARBARA—DUCKWORTH, DANIEL

website: www.chuckdixon.net
E-mail:brunobookstore@gmail.com

Writer—Editor—Publisher—Film Reviewer

Best known for the co-creation of the Batman villain Bane (along with Graham Nolan) as well as the international bestseller graphic novel adaption of *The Hobbit* and for being the most prolific writer of American comics ever. He co-created DC Comics' *Birds of Prey* (along with Jordan B. Gorfinkel) He's worked for every major comics publisher and dozens of independents on titles like *Airboy, Detective Comics, Robin, Nightwing, Savage Sword of Conan, Alien Legion, Moon Knight, SpongeBob Squarepants, G.I. Joe, the Simpsons* and many others. He continues to produce mostly creator-owned comics for a variety of publishers such as *Storming Paradise, Iron Ghost, Winterworld, Joe Frankenstein* and *Go Monster Go!* He also currently writes the popular prose novel series *The Sidewinders, Bad Times* and *Levon Cade* the last of which is currently in preproduction as a television series from Balboa Productions.

DORAN, BARBARA

website: www.sumergoscriptum.com/barbaradoran/
E-mail: (barbardoran@sumergosscriptum.com)

Writer

Author of High Midnight at Knight's Peak, Claws of the Golden Dragon, Wings of the Golden Dragon and Tales of the Golden Dragon, as well as the Wu Dang series; Fist of the Wanderer and Exile of the Wanderer, and a number of short stories, including "The Case of the Counterfeit Secretary"- a Sherlock Holmes/Van Dusen crossover, "Island of the Puppet Master" a Sinbad tale, "City in the Clouds" a Monkey King tale, and "The Book Hunter's Apprentice", a short story appearing in Cirsova Magazine. Barbara's short story, Dust of the Fallen, took second place in Baen Books' Fantasy Award in 2017.

DUCKWORTH, DANIEL
Born—17 Sep 1999
Cordele, GA 31015
United States of America
E-mail: (dduckworth2014@gmail.com)

Writer

New writer at Airship 27. Wrote the Domino Lady's "Three Dead Men"

DYMOWSKI, GORDON
Born—3 March 1968
10320 South Walden Parkway Apt 1W
Chicago, IL 60643
United States of America

website: www.gordondymowski.com
E-mail: (gordon.dymowski@gmail.com)

Writer—Editor

New Pulp writer best known for his work with Pro Se Productions. He won the Pulp Factory Award for Best Pulp Short Story of 2019 for "Knights of the Silver Cross," which appeared in Pro Se Productions' 1950s Western Roundup He also contributed the Black Bat story "One Bullet Too Many" to Pilot Studios' ALWAYS PUNCH NAZIS anthology. He has been published by a variety of companies including Pro Se Productions, Airship 27 Productions, Space Buggy Press, and Last Ember Press. Gordon has also worked as proofreader and copy editor for a variety of publishing companies.

EARL, MAL
Born - 25 Jan 1963
Cumbria
United Kingdom
E-mail: (malcolmear@aol.com)

Writer - Artist

Wrote "Bulletproof Nylon". Self Published alternate history thriller. "Barbary Dove". Western heroine for Piccadilly Publishing. "Stovepipe" - Self Published YA fantasy adventure. And illustrated - "Sherlock Holmes - Picture of Innocence" - cover (Airship 27). "Legends of New Pulp Fiction" - multiple internal illustrations (Airship 27). "Prodigal" - self authored fantasy comic strip - The '77. "Bullhawk" - self authored1920's based vigilante pulp comic strip - Aces Weekly.

ELLIS, MARK
Keamore Cottage
Leap, Co. Cork
Republic of Ireland

website: Markellisink.com
E-mail: (Mark@Markellisink.com)

Writer—Publisher

Art by Kevin James Frear

Mark Ellis is a versatile novelist and comics creator. His numerous credentials in the comics field include critically acclaimed properties such as *Doc Savage, The Wild, Wild West, H.P. Lovecraft's Cthulhu, Star Rangers, Ninja Elite, Nosferatu: Plague of Terror, The Justice Machine, King Solomon's Mines, Death Hawk* and others. With his wife Melissa, he co-authored *The Everything Guide to Writing Graphic Novels.* Under his James Axler pen-name, Mark created the best-selling *Outlanders* novel series for Harlequin Enterprises' Gold Eagle imprint. Published consecutively for over 18 years in various editions, *Outlanders* is the most successful mass market paperback original series of the last 25 years. His other novels include *Cryptozoica* (with Jeff Slemons), *Parallax Prime: Of Dire Chimeras, The Falcon Resurrected, Knightwatch: Invictus X, The Spur* series and entries in The Executioner and Deathlands series. He has been featured in *Starlog, Comics Scene* and *Fangoria* magazines. He has also been interviewed by Robert Siegel for NPR's *All Things Considered.* Mark lives with his wife, best-selling author and photographer Melissa Martin Ellis in rural Ireland.

ERDELAC, EDWARD M. Born—28 Sept, 1975 5419 Hermitage Ave #10 Valley Village, CA 91607 United States of America

website: www.emerdelac.wordpress.com E-mail: (caledre@gmail.com)
Writer
Author of The Merkabah Rider series, Terovolas, Andersonville, Monstrumfuhrer, Buff Tea, Coyote's Trail, Perennial, with stories collected in With Sword And Pistol and Angler In Darkness. Written Star Wars, Sherlock Holmes, James Bond, and Lovecraft.

EVANS, JAMIE
Born—31 May 1974
4325 Latin Lane
Columbus, OH 43220
Unites States of America

website: www.jamie-evans-books.com
E-mail:(jamieevansfiction@gmail.com)

Writer- Publisher

I am a writer of the paranormal and also the publisher of Dark Dossier Magazine. I was born in '74, so I grew up in the 80's (The best time for Movies and TV!) I like Pizza, Beer, Bookstores, Baseball, Movies, Halloween, and Cats. What do my books offer? Easy to read (no need to open up a dictionary), Fast paced, Intriguing and colorful characters, and Snappy fun dialogue. I want my books to entertain and for you to have fun reading them. Think of Hemingway as a Filet Mignon... and me as a diner style cheeseburger. My favorite writers are... Arthur Conan Doyle,

Raymond Chandler, Ernest Hemingway, Elmore Leonard, Hunter S. Thompson, Len Deighton, Edgar Rice Burroughs, & Ray Bradbury. Dark Dossier Magazine is devoted to stories of Aliens, UFOs, Ghosts, Monsters, & Killers. Please visit his websites: www.jamie-evans-books.com and www.darkdossier.com

EVANS, SHANE
14 Silverstream Road
Hora Hora
Whangarei 0110
New Zealand

Artist

Shane Evans is a commercial Illustrator based in Whangarei, New Zealand. Specialist in Illustration and Airbrushing for Print, Murals and Vehicle Art. Producing work in both digital format and traditional mediums, ranging from small jobs up to airbrushed vehicles and murals. Had done work for Airship 27 Productions.

FABI, DEXTER
Born - 6 Nov 1975
989 Shermer Road
Northbrook, IL 60062
United States of America

website: launcelot-dulac.livejournal.com
E-mail: (dexter101@hotmail.com)

Writer - Artist - Reader - Traveler

Raised in the Chicago-area, Dexter writes mystery, science fiction, fantasy, and alternate history. A deep enthusiast of "anything pre-1980," he also enjoys classic films, fiction from the 19th and 20th centuries, old time radio, and vintage book cover art. He has traveled to all continents save South America (which will happen eventually) and is particularly keen on Egypt and its ancient history. He writes for Airship 27 Productions and has published two Sherlock Holmes pastiches in the Sherlock Holmes Consulting Detective line, with more to come. He has also written a baseball story, a Ravenwood story, and others forthcoming. In his leisure time, he is usually at a library or a museum. Dexter started his career as a classroom teacher and is currently a full-time tutor. His favorite pulp novel is The Maltese Falcon and he is also an ardent fan of the original Dark Shadows program by Dan Curtis. In the course of his writing, he was also the recipient of the literary award for Best Short Story for "The Royal Wedding of Oz" at the annual Winkie Convention presented by the International Wizard of Oz Club.

FARNSWORTH, E. W.
534 West RDesert Avenue
Gilbert, Arizona 85233 USA

website www.ewfarnsworth.com
E-mail: (wickengel@aol.com)

Writer - Publisher - Reviewer - Editor

E. W. Farnsworth, whose short stories have won six international first prizes in international competitions, is widely published in the New Pulp arena. Creator of noir detective John Fulghun, PI, for Zimbell House Publishing now in eight volumes, of Ritchie Walgreen, aka Al Katana, now in five linked volumes from Pro Se Productions, of Oliver "Ollie" Handwell in *Bitcoin Fandango*, a picaresque New Pulp police procedural about cryptocurrency crime fighting from GreenmanArizona Press, of spies Salamander and Crow and of the 19th-century southwestern cowgirl Nance, The Bottle Blonde of Albuquerque. He is also "pulp resurrectionist" at large (e.g., Inspector Allhoff in the novel *Dead Cat Bounce* for Pro Se Productions).

FERGUSON, DERRICK
Born—8 Feb. 1959
383 Cumberland Street
Brookly, NY 11238
United States of American

website: https://ferguonink.cm/
E-mail:(DerrickFerguson@gmail.com)

Writer

Best known as the creator of Dillon, Fortune McCall and Sebastian Red. He won the Pulp Factory Award for Best Short Story of 2016 for "Voodah of Thunder Mountain" which appeared in Legends of New Pulp Fiction and the Pulp Ark Award in 2012 for Best Collection: "Four Bullets For Dillon"

FERNLUND, CURTIS
Born—15 May, 1962
1396 Bogart Lane
Eugene, OR 97401
United States of America
E-mail: (kfernland@gmail.com)

Writer—Artist—Editor

Writer best known for his Internet stories and Fanfiction (as carnaj), now a writer for Airship 27 Productions, a leading New Pulp Fiction publisher where he writes the continuing adventures of Kiri the Mist for various publications as well as The Queen of Escapes, his first novel. He received several nominations for his Internet work in various genres and in 2013 he was nominated for the Pulp Ark Awards for Best New Writer and Best New Character: Kiri the Mist.

FINDLEY, PAUL (KEVIN)
Born—28 September 1965
Roseville, CA
United States of America

website: www.linkedin.com/in/kevin-findley-36a20835
E-mail: (kevinfindley@outlook.com)

Writer—Editor

Kevin is a New Pulp writer with multiple tales published in books and magazines from Airship 27, Bold Venture Press, and Pro Se Productions. Work includes stories of classic characters and new creations for Alternative Air Adventures, Domino Lady vol. 1 and 2, Legends of New Pulp Fiction, Police Pulp, Project Moonbase, Pulp Medical, and Purple Scar vol. 2. A 20-year veteran of the U.S. Air Force, Kevin also works as a commercial freelance writer and editor, producing everything from advertising tweets to instruction manuals and textbooks.

FITZSIMONS, MORGAN
Born 1939
United Kingdom

Artist—Author - Teacher

Lived in her beloved Wales, spent some years in Paris, Germany, USA, Africa. Now lives in Cambridgeshire UK. Still an activist for the suffering inequalities and passionate about nurturing and inspiring creativity which underlies everything. She works with pen and ink, watercolour, gouache and acrylic. Currently developing Creative Art Design Studio—CADS, launching new websites late 2020 including fantasy art, animation, and teaching. She illustrates for other people including Airship 27, Occult Detective Magazine, and others. She is known for her detailed fine art, and illustration for projects and characters plus concept art for 3D animation. She is inspired by literature such as ancient Celtic and Norse Myth and writers such as WB Yeats and believes with Albert Einstein 'Imagination is greater than knowledge.' Though knowledge is a close second.

'I've dreamt all my life, dreams that have stayed with me ever after...they've gone through and through me like wine through water and altered the colour of my mind.' Emily Bronte. In 2016 Pulp Ark Awards she won both best cover award and Best artist Award for Dragon Lord's Library from 18th Wall. She is still producing, and all her work is drawn and painted by hand. She has 4 sons one daughter and sixteen grandchildren and 7 great grandchildren and a large extended family most of whom van be found on her face book along with many other well-known world artists and writers.

FIX, ANDY
Born—10 MAR 1970
Cincinnati, OH
United States of America

website: www.facebook.com/Andyfixwriter
E-mail: (andyfixwriter@gmail.com)

Writer

Has following stories published by Airship 27: "Face to Face with Agent Loki", Secret Agent X, Volume 5 "Bloodlines", Legends of New Pulp Fiction "Windy City Widow" (with Jeff Fournier), Aviation Aces "The Devil You Know", Tales of Cape Noire.

FORTENBERRY, THOMAS
Born—23 Aug 1968
13718 Queenswater Dr.
Charlotte, NC 28273
United States of America

website: www.thomasfortenberry.net
E-mail: (thomas@thomasfortenberry.net)

Writer—Editor—Publisher - Reviewer

An historian and internationally published author/editor who has written in almost all fiction genres, poetry, comics, plays/TV/film, and nonfiction. He has won numerous literary awards, has been nominated for the Pushcart Prize, and has also judged many literary contests, including the Georgia Author of the Year Awards and the Robert Penn Warren Prize For Fiction. He published and edited Mindfire for twenty years and co-founded two comic books lines. He writes the continuing adventures of licensed characters (such as Sherlock Holmes, Solar Pons, FEMforce, Silverline, Skyliners) and original characters (such as Atlas, Dr. Darke, Shadowchaser, Champions, Queen City Knights, Guardians, Alexander Drake, Blackjackets, Captain Redeagle, Private Graves, Lady Incognita, Sharlokh and Watt-ZENN, Doc Wilder, The Custodian, Mad Monsignor, Aaron Skullsplitter, etc.)

FORTIER, RON

Born—5 Nov 1946
6508 Fossil Crest Dr.
Fort Collins, CO 80525
United States of America

website: www.airship27.com
E-mail: (airship27@comcast.net)

Writer—Editor—Publisher- Reviewer

Comics and pulps writer/editor is best known for his work on the Green Hornet comic series and Terminator—Burning Earth with Alex Ross. He won the Pulp Factory Award for Best Pulp Short Story of 2011 for "Vengeance Is Mine," which appeared in Moonstone's The Avenger—Justice Inc. and in 2012 for "The Ghoul," from the anthology Monster Aces. He is the Managing Editor of Airship 27 Productions, a leading New Pulp Fiction publisher and writes the continuing adventures of both his own character, Brother Bones—the Undead Avenger and the classic pulp hero, Captain Hazzard—Champion of Justice. In 2017, he was awarded the first Pulp Grand Master by the Pulp Factory. Fortier also writes the highly popular Pulp Fiction Reviews blog.

FOSTER, LUKE

United States of America

website: www.imlukefoster.com
E-mail: (lukejfoster@gmail.com)

Writer

Comics and fiction writer published online and in magazines in the US and UK. He has written stories in nearly every genre including horror, crime, comedy, fantasy, and science fiction. His first story, "Get to the River," was published in StoryHack Action & Adventure Magazine #3. As an independent comic creator, he wrote and drew the all-ages comic book series "Doctor Bananas: Monkey Magician" and the comedy/horror anthology "Spookytown."

FOSTER, NEIL T.

Born - 5 March 1963
Queensland, Australia
E-mail: (foster.62@bigpond.com)

Artist / Illustrator

Has pencilled, inked and painted cover art for various independent Australian comics as well as providing art for action figure boxes and sci-fi fanzines. In 2003 brought Planet of the Apes back to comic book form as penciller, inker and cover artist of the highly regarded graphic novel 'Beware The Beast', a fan collaboration serialised on various web sites at the time.

Cover and interior artist for different horror and sci-fi magazines including The Corpse Magazine, Black Petals and popular fantasy magazine 'Tales Of The Talisman', contributing interior art for almost every issue until its hiatus. Has so far contributed interior illustrations for 3 Airship 27 releases; 'Dan Fowler: G-Man Vol. 2', 'Green Lama - Mystic Warrior Vol.1' and the western novel 'Gun Glory'.

FOURNIER, JEFF "Venture"
Born—1970;s
Cleveland, Ohio
United States of America
E-mail: (Jeffventure@hotmail.com)

Writer

Non fiction and multi-genre pulp writer. Jeff has primarily been published with Airship 27 with Sword and Sorcery (Sinbad and the Isle of Madness in their Sinbad series anthology) and the creation of the Printer's Devil in the 1930's mystery man type for Airship's New Pulp Anthology. He is also a reviewer that has been published on several print and E-magazines for outdoors and gear reviews. He co writes with long time friend and fellow author Andy Fix, their latest being an air tale about lovers involved in World War II military aviation.

FRANKLIN, ERIK
Born—12 March, 1989
Kent, WA

website: www.erikonpaper.com

E-mail: (erik.franklin12@yahoo.com)

Writer—Artist

A pulp writer and comic illustrator, Erik is known for his work with Airship 27. He has worked on many award nominated books including Sherlock Holmes, Consulting Detective vol. 9, The Wraith Volume One, Towers of Metropolis and Major Sabbath. In the world of comics he has worked on the classic Golden Age character Blue Bolt and written for the title Girl Commandos for Lucky Comics and Skyscraper for The Surprising Universe.

FRENCH, JOHN L.
Born—25 February 1954
Baltimore, MD
United States of America

website: none at this time
E-mail: (jfrenchfam@aol.com)

Writer—Editor

A retired crime scene investigator from Baltimore with over forty years' experience, John is a short story writer/editor who got his start writing pulp for Tom Johnson's magazines. Two of his stories in his book *Past Sins* were cited as among the best hardboiled stories in the years they were published. His pulp characters include Frank Devlin (*The Devil of Harbor City*), The Nightmare (*The Nightmare Strikes & Shadows and Brimstone*), The Grey Monk (*Souls on Fire*) and Simon Tombs (*The Magic of Simon Tombs.*) He is also the creator of the Bianca Jones - Monster Hunter series. His non-series crime fiction can be found in *The Last Redhead.* John had edited/coedited *Bad Cop No Donut*, *To Hell in a Fast Car*, *Mermaids 13*, *Camelot 13*, and *With Great Power* ... He has also edited books for Padwolf Publishing.

FYLES, MIKE
Born - 17 May 1955
20 Seabridge Road
Newcastle under Lyme
Staffordshire
ST5 2HT
United Kingdom

E-mail: (mike.fyles@gmail.com)

Illustrator

Narrative illustrator best known for cover art work on a range of New Pulp titles (Moonstone Press, The Pulp Obscure line: Pro-Se Productions, Ucronic Tales, Airship 27, Fight Card Press, Thrillville Press, Lockport Steampunk and TimePiece Press). Pulp characters depicted include The Green Lama, The Black Bat, Domino Lady, Kolchak, The Man in Purple, Thunder Jim Wade, Armless O'Neil, Lynn Lash, Semi Dual, Richard Knight, The Eagle, The Griffin, The Whirlwind, Señorita Scorpion, Diamondstone, Jim Anthony, Green Ghost, Moon Man, Foster Fade, Dan Fowler Major Lacy, Shadow Legion, Zeppelin Tales, Sherlock Holmes (Blood to the Bone, Consulting Detective, Investigates, Queensbury Justice and A Congression of Pallbearers), The Iron Fist of Ned Kelly, King of the Outback, Rumble in the Jungle, and Eby Stokes of Special Branch. Mike won the Pulp Factory Award for Best Interior Illustrations for Green Lama Unbound (2010) and was commissioned by Marvel Comics to produce cover art for Iron Man Noir and the Grim Hunt story arc in Amazing Spiderman (2011).

GALLAGHER, BRIAN
London
United Kingdom Twitter - @bgxyz

Writer
Brian Gallagher has written for the *Tales of the Shadowmen* and *Vampire Almanac* anthologies, published by Black Coat Press. For *Tales of the Shadowmen*, he wrote a series about Captain Vampire, the character created by Marie Nizet in 1879. From Volume 10 through to 16 of *Tales of the Shadowmen*, he revived Captain Vampire, charting his exploits from 1830 to 2024. A collection of all the stories, *The Return of Captain Vampire*, is due to be published in late 2020 by Black Coat Press, following from a French version in 2019. He is currently working on a new series for *Tales of the Shadowmen*, featuring Gustav Le Rouge's creation, the classic French pulp

villain Doctor Cornelius.

GASTON, D K
Michigan
United States of America

website: www.dkgaston.com

Writer

D K Gaston is an Information Technology professional and author. His debut novel, XIII, features bounty hunter Avery Hudson. He went on to publish over dozens of books written in various genres and formats. Among his works are the Taurus Moon and Joe Hooks series as well as many stand-alone action and adventure novels. In his youth, he'd spent hours creating heroes and villains with the dream of one day working in the comic book industry. That didn't happen yet. But his dream of writing fantastic characters, and fighting the forces of evil didn't end there. He has been able to bring some of his past creations to life in many of his novels. D K Gaston is currently working on his next novel.

GATES, DON
Born—4 Jun 1974
Ontario
Canada

website - http://challengerstorm.blogspot.com/
E-mail: (MARDLverse@yahoo.com)

Writer

New Pulp writer, best known for his Challenger Storm series published by Airship 27 Productions. Has also had short stories appearing in Legends of New Pulp Fiction as well as volume 2 of Tales from the Hanging Monkey (both titles also published by Airship 27 Productions).

GENTILE, JOE
Born—2 June 1963

1655 S. Pinecreek Dr.
Lockport, IL 60441
United States of America

website: www.moonstonebooks.com
E-mail: (contact-us@moonstonebooks.com)

Writer—Editor—Publisher
Comics and pulp writer best known for his work: Buckaroo Banzai, Kolchak the Nightstalker, Zorro, Captain Action, Werewolf the Apocalypse, The Avenger, Sherlock Holmes, and The Spider. As the Publisher of Moonstone, also brought to life projects featuring: The Phantom, Vampire the Masquerade, The Green Hornet, The Black Bat, The Green Ghost, Honey West, Airboy, Domino Lady, The Green Lama, and so many more.

GICK, GREG
Born—23 Nov 1968
Indiana
United States of America

Writer

New pulp writer best known for his work on the GREEN HORNET, TALES OF THE SHADOWMEN, and Airship 27's

Art by Morgan Fitzsimons

MARS MCOCY, SECRET AGENT X and MEN OF MYSTERY anthologies. Creator of pulp villain The Brown Recluse.

GILL, JERRY
Born 12-20-48
POBox 6495
Kaneohe HI 96744
United States of America

website - http://www.vicplanet.com
E-mail: jerrygillauthor@gmail.com

Writer

New pulp adventure writer best known for the series The Incredible Adventures of Vic Challenger, about a reincarnated cave girl who battles bad guys and cryptids in the 1920s. He served eight valuable years in the U.S. Army, then wasted - er, attended the school of life - many years in such boring endeavors as hospital Director of Staff Development and organizational specialist, then years publishing medical coding books. Finally, he gave in to the urge to write adventure, which he first dreamed of when thirteen. That was that. Bridges were burned. As of this writing (mid 2020) volume ten in the series and other non-series projects are scheduled for later in the year.

GILMOUR, KANE
Born—8 May 1971
PO Box 1285
Montpelier, VT 05602
United States of America

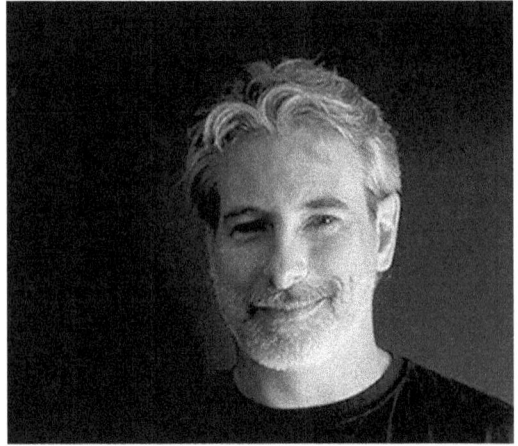

website: www.kanegilmour.com
E-mail:: kane@kanegilmour.com

Writer—Editor—Publisher

International bestselling author of *The Crypt of Dracula.* Gilmour has written web comics and print comics, and he has contributed short stories to several anthologies. He collaborated with Jeremy Robinson on several books, including on the Jack Sigler / Chess Team thriller series. He also edited and contributed a short story to Scott P. Vaughn's 2014 New Pulp Awards-nominated anthology, *Warbirds of Mars: Stories of the Fight!*

GLENN, TEEL JAMES
Born—3 March Nov 1955
27 50 (RS)
Weehawken NJ
United States of America

website – TheUrbanSwashbuckler.com
E-mail: (tjglenn@aol.com)

Writer

For 45 years has been an actor and stunt-man— most known for playing Vega in *Street Fighter: the later years*, and was Dr. Strange for Marvel Comics for 7 years in personal appearances. He is known for his various pulp/new pulp era original book series including Dr. Shadows, Jon Shadows, Gideon Synn, Maxi & Moxie Donovan, The Renfairies, The Exceptionals, Dr. Argent and the Bob Howard Adventures. He has also written 'classic' pulp series characters, including Sherlock Holmes, The Eagle, Alias the Whirlwind, Lynn Lash, Gunmaster and Airboy. He has written for a wide range of magazines including Mad, Weird Tales, Pulp Adventures, Mystery Weekly, Sherlock Holmes Mystery, Fantasy Tales, Steampunk Tales, Blazing Adventures, Black Belt and Deadly Hands of Kung Fu.

Winner of the 2012 Pulp Ark 'Best Author of the Year.' Epic Ebook Award finalist. P&E winner 'Best Thriller Novel', "Best Steampunk Short", Multiple finalist "Best Fantasy short stories," Collection" Member HWA, MWA, HNS, ITWA.

HALL, SHANNON
Born—8 March 1975
P.O. Box 775
Cartersville, Ga. 30120
United States of America
E-mail: (shameous@bellsouth.net)

Artist—Writer

Comics and Pulp Artist/ writer best known for his cover and interior Illustrations in such works as Lance Star v.3 , Mars McCoy v.2, Golden Gang v.2, Mr. Cynic, Legends of New Pulp Fiction, Restless cover and also the cover of The Persona. He is currently working on several creator owned projects that he is writing and drawing.

HAMMOND, TED

website: www.tedhammond.com

Artist

Ted Hammond has been creating art for over two decades for a wide variety of clients and projects! His work has been seen in books, magazines, graphic novels, ads, posters and kid's books just to name a few. He received his start doing illustration work for fitness magazines and books back in the nineties . It was through his work there he drew the attention of fitness guru, Jack Lalanne. He illustrated several projects for Jack and also designed Jack's grave stone in Forest Lawn cemetery. Ted has also done extensive work creating television story-boards for many well known clients including Tylenol and Reebok and Nike. In 2019 he was awarded Best Cover Art by Pulp Factory for Jezebel Johnson: Mourning Star. Currently, he is creating a graphic novel for the DEA museum in Arlington VA.

HANCOCK, TOMMY
Born—6 June 1972
Melbourne, Arkansas
United States of America

website: www.prose-press.com
E-mail: editorinchief@prose-press.com

Writer—Editor—Publisher—Reviewer

Steeped in pulp magazines, old radio

shows, and all things of that era's pop culture, Tommy Hancock lives in Arkansas with his wonderful wife and three children and obviously not enough to do. He is Partner in and Editor in Chief for Pro Se Productions, is an organizer of the New Pulp Movement, and has worked as an editor for various companies, including Moonstone, winning the 2019 Pulp Factory Award for editing YOURS TRULY, JOHNNY DOLLAR. He has written for various companies, including Airship 27, Mechanoid Press, Pulpwork Press, Dark Oak, and Moonstone. He also won the 2012 Pulp Ark Award for Best Short story for 'Lucky', his entry in Radio Archives' NIGHTBEAT anthology. He is also a reviewer of books at www.facebook.com/Bibliorati.

HANSEN, NANCY A.
Born—April 3, 1957
Lives in beautiful, rural Eastern Connecticut
United States of America

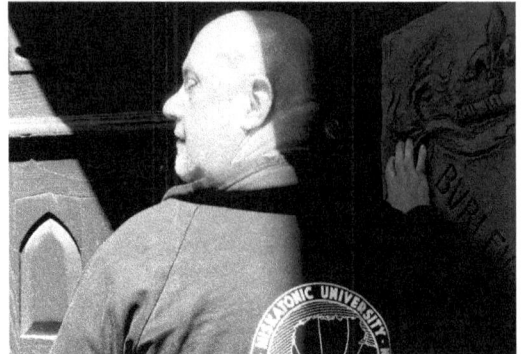

Amazon Author Page—amazon.com/author/nancyahansen
Also easily found on Facebook and Twitter
Blogs- http://nancyahansen.blogspot.com/ and http://magicdragonverse.blogspot.com/
E-mail: hansennancya@gmail.com

Writer—Editor - Reviewer

Always an avid reader and a prolific writer for over 30 years as well, Nancy Hansen is best known for her fantasy and action adventure tales in multiple genres; all with pulp pacing. She currently has 19 novels in print and more waiting in the wings, along with numerous short stories. Her work has been published by New Pulp publishers Pro Se Productions, Airship 27, Mechanoid Press, and Flinch Books, and she will occasionally do a short story charity piece if you ask nicely. Because of her continual output, Pro Se has given Nancy her own imprint, *Hansen's Way*. Her popular Jezebel Johnston pirate series from Airship 27 is now up to 6 books in print with more to come, and the first 4 Jezebel Johnston books were collected in an Airship 27 premiere omnibus edition, JEZEBEL JOHNSTON: BIRTH OF A BUCCANEER. Nancy writes from a house built in 1770, situated on 29 country acres of an old dairy farm, where she lives with an eclectic cast of family members and one very spoiled dog.

HARDIN, CHAD
Born—1974
United States of America

website: chadhardinart.com
E-mail: hardinart@hotmail.com

Cover Artist / Illustrator

Award winning Pulp Cover Artist. Also a noted comic book artist popular for his work on DC's Harlee Quinn series.

HARRIS, MICAH S.
Born—19 May 1961
North Carolina
United States of America

website (1) www.minorprofitpress.com
website (2) www.aarastad.com
E-mail: (MHa6106@aol.com)

Writer—Film Historian - Publisher

Micah S. Harris is an award-winning author whose work has been published in both his native United States and abroad. With artist Michael Gaydos, he created the Image Comics graphic novel Heaven's War which pits the Oxford Inklings against occultist Aleister Crowley. In the New Pulp genre, Harris has written "On the Periphery of Legend" (Jim Anthony -the Hunters) and "A Gathering of Peacocks" (Ghost Boy) for Airship 27 Productions as well as several short stories for Black Coat Press' Tales of the Shadowmen. He won the 2016 Pulp Ark Award for best novel for Ravenwood, the Stepson of Mystery: Return of the Dugpa (Airship 27 Productions). His Cthulhu Mythos story for 18th Wall Productions, "Tatterdemalion In Gray," has been called "a powerful piece of fiction...a stunning idea...that deserves multiple rereads" (Sci-fi and Fantasy Reviewer Blog). Also, in a Cthulhu vein, Harris is the chronicler of The Eldritch New Adventures of Becky Sharp. He has recently focused on launching his epic fantasy series The Chronicles of Aarastad for his own Minor Profit Press, beginning with Portrait of a Snow Queen.

HARVEY, COLIN B
London, UK

website: www.cbharvey.com
E-mail: (colinharvey@colinharvey.net)

Writer—Narrative Designer

Colin B Harvey is a British writer working across different media. He is currently Lead Writer with Sony's PlayStation London Studio. He co-wrote the screenplay for the Virtual Reality video game *Blood and Truth*, a London-set gangster thriller starring Colin Salmon, Natasha Little and Felix Scott. Prior to this he wrote the screenplay for the World War Two game *Sniper Elite 4*. He is the author of the novel *Sinbad and the Warriors of Forever* for Airship 27 and *Dead Kelly* for Abaddon Books. Colin's other work includes licensed material for the *Doctor Who* and *Highlander* ranges published by Big Finish Productions, the *Judge Dredd* roleplaying game and short fiction for Moonstone Books' *Black Bat* series. His gothic short fiction won the first Pulp Idol award in 2006, jointly conferred by the British science fiction and fantasy magazine *SFX* and the publisher Gollancz. His comic work includes material for the British comics *2000AD* and *Commando*. Colin is the author of *Fantastic Transmedia*, a non-fiction book published by Palgrave-Macmillan exploring crossmedia science fiction and fantasy franchises such as *Star Wars*, *The Lord of the Rings* and the Marvel Cinematic Universe. Colin is currently a Visiting Professor with the Manchester School of Writing.

HARVEY, RICH
Born—1968
Sunrise, FL
United States of America

website: www.boldventurepress.com
E-mail: (boldventurepress@comcast.net)

Writer—Editor—Publisher—Reviewer

Best known for editing and publishing *Zorro: The Complete Pulp Adventures* by Johnston McCulley — the first complete collection of the famous character's adventures. Also, his anthology *Compliments of the Domino Lady* by Lars Anderson (2004, newly illustrated by the legendary Steranko) launched the "Domino Lady revival." Currently publishing average of 24 books (or more) every year — both "New Pulp" and classic reprints.

HATCHER, GREG

Born—13 Nov 1961
6508 Fossil Crest Dr.
Burien, Wa 98166
United States of America

website: http://atomicjunkshop.com/category/hatcher/
E-mail: (ghatcher79@gmail.com)

Writer—Editor—Reviewer

Writer and columnist for over a decade at Comic Book Resources before moving on to his current gig at the Atomic junk Shop. Contributing editor at **With** magazine for eleven years where he won the Higher Goals Award for Children's Writing three times, once for fiction and twice for non-fiction. Has contributed to numerous "new pulp" hero anthologies like Airship 27's Domino Lady, Green Ghost, Black Bat, and Moon Man collections, among others.

Also a lifelong mystery enthusiast, Greg has done Nero Wolfe and Sherlock Holmes pastiches for a variety of publishers. In addition to all that Greg has been teaching Young Authors for 6th, 7th and 8th graders since 2009, long enough to see several grads turn pro themselves.

HAYES, JEFF

Born—4 June 1962
2600 Bowen Street
Leander, Texas 78641
United States of America

website: www.plasmafiregraphics.com
E-mail: (Jeffrey.hayes@plasmafiregraphics.com)

Illustrator / Graphic Designer

Completing cover illustration art and title design work under the company name Plasmafire Graphics and as Jeffrey Ray Hayes, he is best known for his work on over 125 new pulp print and eBook covers published by Pro Se Press, hundreds of freelance book covers for indie authors and box art for audio drama productions, as well as a number of one-sheet movie posters for independent film productions. Nominated in 2015 for the Pulp Factory Best Pulp Cover Award for his work on Gary Phillips' "Hollis P.I." (Pro Se Press), Nominated in 2016 for the Pulp Ark New

Pulp Award Best Artist and nominated in 2016 for the Pulp Ark New Pulp Award Best Cover for Nikki Nelson-Hicks' "Jake Istenhegyi: The Accidental Detective Vol. 1" and nominated in 2019 for the The Wild Bunch Film Festival - Best Movie Poster for his one-sheet movie poster art on Jerry Robbins' screenplay "Catch the Bullet." Hayes continues to accept commissions from indie authors and publishers for cover art and title design.

HILL, GRAHAM
Born—Feb 1965
1 Fairview, Barnstaple
Devon, EX31 1JR
United Kingdom

E-mail: (Graham@amgrafcomics.co.uk)

Artist—Painter
Comics, pulp and book cover painter, Completed work for many publishers worldwide including Airship 27, Wetta-Sunnyside, IDW / Yoe Books, Bluewater / Tidlewave comics, EditoraDTX, Estronho. Other cover work for small press publishers such as Bloke's Terrible Tomb of Terror, Ape Chronicles, Simian Scrolls. 2018 saw the publication of the award-winning "A Invaso Dos Macacos" from author Saulo Adami and Brazillian publisher EditoraDTX which featured around ten fully painted illustration, covers and end-papers by Graham. Probably best known for his painted portrait covers for many biographical comics, David Bowie, Freddy Mercury, John Lennon, plus many more. Originally earned a First class BA Hons degree in Fine Art when he was much younger and had more hair.

HINKLE, CLAYTON
Born 26 Feb. 1957
498 Elm Ave.
Chula Vista, CA 91910
United States of America

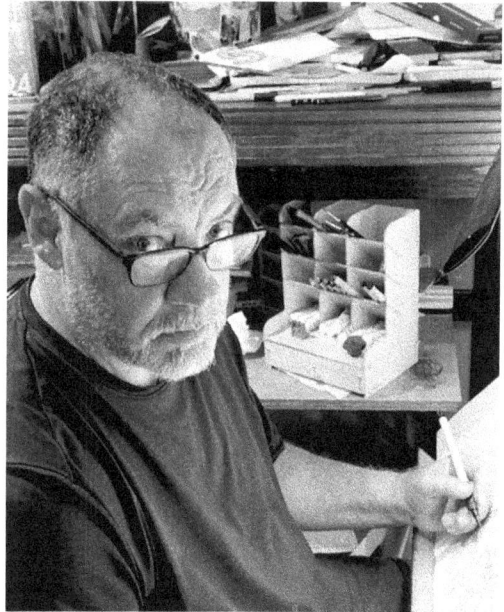

E-mail: (gombuk99@yahoo.com)

Artist - Comic Creator - Cartoonist

Self-taught artist who grew up on paper-backs (most of which were pulp reprints) and comics. Very influenced by classic writers like Robert E. Howard and Edgar Rice Burroughs, and others too numerous to list, as well as artists and writers of Marvel, DC, and many other comic companies. Artist favorites and influencers include, but are not limited to, Frank Frazetta (my all-time favorite), Roy Krenkal, John Buscema, Jack Kirby, Jack Davis, Mort

Drucker, Mark Shultz, Bernie Wrightston, Jeff Jones, and many others too numerous to name. Illustrated many books in the New Pulp field, as well as fanzine work, created and wrote, drew, and lettered two comics, Thro-Bak and Tonga of Lemuria, (with permission from the estate of Lin Carter), and from time to time created quite a few gag cartoons, the best of which will someday be collected in a book, hopefully!

HOPEN, STUART
Born—5 June, 1953

website: stuarthopen.com
E-mail: (stuarthopen@gmail.com)

Writer—Artist– Reviewer

Stuart Hopen is the leading authority on *The Twilight Patrol*, a rare and obscure pulp magazine from 1935 reprinted by Bold Venture Press, though he is not to be confused with the actual author and illustrator of that series, credited to a "house name" that eerily and coincidently is also "Stuart Hopen". He has written comic books published by D.C. Comics, Marvel, Fantagraphics, Eclipse, and *Amazing Comics*. His critical writing has been published by *Rain Taxi Review of Books* and the *Comics Journal*. His techno-

gothic space opera, *Warp Angel* (Tor Books, 1992), has been reissued in a new, revised edition from Misentchanted Press. Other works include the *Remembrance Acres,* a story cycle from Bold Venture Press, *The Flick,* a post-modern gothic romance serialized in Fiction365, and *Cannibals,* an illustrated novel.

HOUSEL, MICHAEL
Born — 23 Jan 1964
927 Park Av
Trenton, NJ 08629

Blog http://bizarrechats.blogspot.com/
E-mail: — (mikehousel@hotmail.com)

Writer — Reviewer

Michael F. Housel commenced his writing career with toy and model-kit reviews for magazines in the '90s, but later branched out with short stories and novels. He has worked since 2016 with Ron Fortier and Rob Davis' Airship 27 Productions, contributing to the New Pulp domain. For Airship 27, Housel created the character, the Persona (aka Michael Mansford), a masked crusader who fights evildoers by absorbing (and tossing back) their dastardly deeds, so that they may experience the effects of their actions. The Persona has thus far been featured in the novels, "Enter—the Persona!" & "The Persona: Green-Fleshed Fiends." Airship 27 has also published Housel's novella, THE HYDE SEED, about

Art by Steve Bryant

a forlorn boxer who gains a second chance at life by facing his fiercest opponent—himself. In addition, Housel has contributed to Airship 27's RAVENWOOD, STEPSON OF MYSTERY, VOL IV and THE PURPLE SCAR , VOL IV. Housel publishes weekly for his blog, "bizarrechats", writing book, movie, music and artwork reviews. He also guest contributes for Main Enterprises' WHAT EVER! Magazine.

HOUSTON, LEE Jr.
Born: 5 March, 1962
Connecticut
United States of America

website: http://leehoustonjr.blogspot.com/
(Filling Blank Spaces, my writer's blog)
E-mail:: authorhoustonjrlee@gmail.com

Writer - Editor

Lee Houston, Junior (or Jr., depending upon the whims of the cover letterer) is a writer and editor of various genres within New Pulp. Starting out with Pro Se Press since the company's inception in 2010 as story editor for Fantasy and Fear and Pro Se Presents magazines, Lee is also the writer-creator of Hugh Monn, Private Detective and Alpha the superhero, with several other short stories published in various anthologies. While his complete bibliography can be found on his Amazon author's page, Lee's other creative credits include work for Airship 27, contributing to and co-editing the Super Swingin' Hero 1968 Special with Jim Beard from Mechanoid Press, editing Victoria Pagac's comic book mini-series Raye Knight: Spellbound from Indy Planet, and serving as the Editor-In-Chief of The Free Choice E-zine (www.thefreechoice.info) since 2005. In what he laughing refers to as his "spare" time, Lee is an avid reader of classic pulps, science-fiction, detective/mystery stories, fantasy, and comic books. Besides via his writer's blog and E-mail: listed above, Lee also maintains contact with readers via Facebook and Twitter, and finds it hard to talk about himself in the third person.

HOWLAND, WHITNEY hueydusk@gmail.com

Writer—Reviewer

Pulp novelist and serial writer. He is best known for stories about his beloved clown detective Huey Dusk that he wrote for Untreed Reads. He has also written Johnny Nickle -Trouble Follows, a novella for Pro Se Press. Along with that he has written The Phantom Detective - Campaign of Destruction, and Dan Fowler-The Bloody Murdocks for Airship 27. Lastly, he has self- published The Doomsday Gizmo(A Lowell Pike Thriller) which can be found on Amazon.com. He is currently in partnership with another filmmaker and playwright and they are working on a podcast of Huey Dusk. Other future projects include a Masked Rider story for Airhship 27, as well another Huey Dusk story for Untreed Reads.

JACKSON, MICHAEL DEAN
Born—13 Jan1965
3090 20th Avenue NE
Salmon Arm, BC V1E 1M9
Canada

website: mdjackson.artstation.com
E-mail: (mikenfran3@hotmail.com)

Artist—Writer—Publisher - Webmaster

Canadian Science fiction, fantasy and horror illustrator and artist, his artwork has appeared on numerous book covers, and on the covers and inside pages of various magazines including the current revival of Amazing Stories Magazine. His artwork has been used on the covers of books from Pulpwork Press, Rogue Blades Press and Rage Machine Books, among others, and his black and white illustrations have appeared in publications from Airship 27 as well as recently from The Experimenter Publishing Company. His work has been featured on various websites including Darkworlds Quarterly, a website that he designed and currently maintains as webmaster. He was the co-publisher of Darkworlds Quarterly Magazine, a non-fiction online publication, providing illustrations as well as design and layout of each issue. He also wrote many of the articles about science fiction, fantasy and art. He wrote about similar subjects for the Amazing Stories Magazine Website as well as at the now defunct Heroicology Website. Before that he was the co-publisher and art director of Dark Worlds Magazine, a pulp inspired print-on-demand fiction magazine. His work garnered him a co-nomination for a Pulp Ark Award in 2012.

JACKSON, CHARLES LEE II
Born 06-26-1950

website: www.CLJII.com
E-mail: (cljii@CLJII.com)

Writer—Artist - Editor.

Mr. Jackson, who had overcome a childhood disability to work in the motion picture industry, moved on to magazine publishing, including ground-level comics, before turning, in 1991, to prose. His "Amazing Adventures" magazine featured short stories, novelettes, and serialized novels starring super-heroes, adventurers, cowboys of yesteryear, spacemen of tomorrow, and more, prefiguring what is now called "New Pulp". Begun in book format in 2006, these stories, reprints augmented by new adventures, comprise "The Emperor's Secret

Files" series, a shared-continuity collection slated to number 100 books of which over a third are now available under the "Digital Parchment" imprint, digitally and on paper, featuring characters including Solara, Cat's-Eye, Fireball, the Trail Riders, the space cops of Star Service, and the central figure of the series, The Emperor, a sort of plainclothes superman whose exploits combine science fiction, fantasy, spy, and thriller elements. A noted film scholar, Mr. Jackson has also produced a number of review columns, film-history articles, and books on the serials and series pictures of Hollywood's "Golden Age". For his contributions to science fiction, he is a recipient of the "Forrest J Ackerman Award" for service to the genre. He is at present working to complete his "Secret Files" series and a non-fiction history of serials, in his secret headquarters somewhere near Hollywood, USA.

JANSSENS, KEN
Born—20 May 1974
102 Pembridge Bay
Winnipeg, MB R2M 4h4

website: https://kenjanssens1.wixsite.com/kenjanssens
E-mail: (janssensken@hotmail.com)

Writer—Screenplays—Comics

Ken is a published comic book writer, a produced film and television screenwriter, a published novelist, a produced playwright, a produced radio playwright, and a published, two-time award-nominated prose writer. His YA novel "The Sisters Arcana" was published by Pro Se Press and he has had several pulp stories published (the most notable being in his "Aloha McCoy", "Sherringford Bell", and "Cerberus Clan" series). His published comic book works include "Hindsight" for Comixology, "The Last Hunt" for Amigo Comics, "Robin The Hood" and "Sherlock Holmes: Victorian Knights" for Bluewater, and his on-

line graphic novel "Caleb Elsewhere" on Webtoons. Three of his films—the feature "The Return" (starring Richard Harmon from "The 100") and the shorts "Orion" and "Gutshot"—are currently in post-production.

JENKINS, JOEL
Born—9 March 1967
Marysville, WA
United States of America

website –www.joeljenkins.net
E-mail: (airship27@comcast.net)

Writer

Joel Jenkins is a prolific author writing in a variety of genres, but all his novels and stories containing elements of action, adventure, and the vibrant prose associated with the New Pulp movement. He is perhaps best known for his sword and science fiction Dire Planet series, chronicling the adventures of astronaut Garvey Dire on a prehistoric Mars. Other notable characters include the vampire hunter Damon St. Cloud, the genetic experiment Max Damage, assassin Monica Killingsworth, the gunslinging rock musicians Gantlet Brothers, dispossessed king Strommand Greattrix, and Native American gunfighter Lone Crow. Genres Jenkins works in include Western, Weird-Western, Sword & Science Fiction, Space Opera, Biography, Action-Adventure, Horror, and Fantasy. His series work to date is comprised of Dire Planet, the Greattrix Chronicles, Barclay Salvage, Monica Killingsworth, Tales from the City of Bathos, Lone Crow, Weird Worlds of Joel Jenkins, the Gantlet Brothers, Denbrook Supernatural, and Damage Inc.

JOHNSON, KEVIN
Born—6 Feb 1970
1312 Canoe Creek Dr
Colorado Springs Co 80906
United States of America

website: www.kevjart.com
E-mail: (kvnjohnson12@gmail.com)

Illustrator—Painter—3D artist

Comics Illustrator and painter. Best known for his work as an illustrator on" Black Lion", a four-part comic mini-series, with writer Ron Fortier for Red Bud Studios. Illustrated book covers for Airship27's Sindad, " The New Voyages", and "Jezebel Johnston " Birth of a Buccaneer" . Trained, and mentored as a student for six years, with the world renowned artist, and Hall of Fame Society of Illustrators 2020 inductee Thomas Blackshear.

JONES, R.A.
Born—12 March, 1953
Tulsa, Oklahoma
United States of America
E-mail:(prezjones@juno.com)

Writer—Editor—Reviewer

R.A. Jones began his professional career writing for the popular comics fan magazine *Amazing Heroes.* For that work he received the Best Writer About Comics award in one of fan magazine *Comics Buyer's Guide*'s annual fan polls. He has also been a columnist and movie/TV reviewer for various newspapers and magazines. He soon transitioned over from reviewing to writing and editing comics series himself. His work as a comic book writer includes contributions to Marvel (*Wolverine/ Captain America; Weapon X*); DC (*Showcase '95*); Dark Horse (*Harlan Ellison's Dream Corridor*) and Image (*Bulletproof Monk; Automaton*). Much of his comics work was produced for Malibu Comics, including *Scimidar; Dark Wolf; Fist of God; Ferret; The Protectors* and various Ultraverse titles. He is currently writing two new comic book series—*Twilight Grimm* and *Divinity*—for Silverline Comics. Having been raised on the adventures of such pulp icons as Tarzan, Doc Savage and Conan the Barbarian, R.A, eventually transitioned to writing pulp-influenced prose in his own right. Among the dozen books he has written or co-written are *Deathwalker; Scimidar; Gun Glory; Motor City Manhunt; Global Star; The Equation; Comanche Blood* and a series of novels featuring the Golden Age Centaur Comics superheroes: *The Steel Ring; The Twilight War* and *The House of Souls.* The Toy and Action Figure Museum in Pauls Valley, Oklahoma inducted R.A. into its Oklahoma Cartoonists Hall of Fame.

JUN, RICH
Born—9/8/1977
Madison Wisconsin
United States of America

website: Instagram handle: shooonuff
E-mail: (shooonuff@gmail.com)

Writer—Artist

Rich Jun is an aspiring comic book illustrator and a professional doctor of optometry. He spent most of his formative years pouring over comic books. He continues to worship the likes of Art Adams, John Buscema, John Byrne and Jim Lee. He majored in drawing and painting at Loyola University in Chicago and studied at the Art Institute of Chicago. After graduation, Rich worked odd jobs but struggled to crack into the art world.

He went to graduate school to become an eye doctor in New York City. Rich has spent the last ten years treating patients from eye diseases and preventing blindness. All the while, he continued his affair with comic books and action figures. After moving to Madison Wi, Rich met Jeff Butler, while attending one of his comic art classes. He studied with Jeff for two years. Under Jeff's tutelage, his aspirations have reignited.

He has the privilege to work on characters like MoonMan, Jim Anthony, Captain Jain Marlee and Sam Dunne! Rich is grateful and thrilled to work under the incredible Airship 27 with Ron Fortier and Rob Davis.

JUSTICE, MARK
Born July, 1967
Shefflield Village, OH 44054
United States of American

E-mail: (gojifanmark@yahoo.com
Writer

Pulp, non-fiction, and genre fiction. In 2019, he published two novels, one the first in a series of grim and violent pulp westerns - *Gauge Black: Hell's Revenge*, the other a cozy mystery—*'Twas the Week After Christmas*. He has two more pulp series in the works, an action/adventure homage to The Phantom—*Death's Head*, and a horror anthology inspired in part by Lovecraft—*Chatham Dark*. Much of his non-fiction writing has been published in *G-FAN* magazine and focuses on various cultural aspects in kaiju movies. In 2011, he was nominated for a Rondo Hatten Classic Horror Award for Best Article for his essay "Save the Earth: Ecological Messages in Toho's Giant Monster Movies."

KARFORMA, KAUSHIK
Born—12 Dec 1976
Kolkata, West Bengal, India

Twitter—@KaushikKarforma

Author

Kaushik lives and works in Kolkata, a city in eastern India, where he spends whatever time he can spare from raising a rambunctious five-year old daughter and a demanding day job reading spy-thrillers, science-fiction, and comics, and watching movies and TV series. Some of his favorite authors—across mediums—include Donald Westlake, Robert Ludlum, Eric van Lustbader, Ed Brubaker, Andy Diggle, Ed Greenwood, Max Alan Collins, and Alistair MacLean. He also occasionally writes. His first, and so far, only, published writing is a Secret Agent X story from Airship 27. He is now plotting a number of stories in science-fiction and crime genres and will get down to writing them soon. A lifelong progressive and liberal, he hopes to do his bit in combating authoritarianism and bigotry through his writing.

KATO, GARY
Born: December 9, 1949
Address: 1013 7th Avenue
Honolulu, HI 96816
United States of America

E-mail:: jiggyhono@hotmail.com

Illustrator - Letterer - Writer

Gary Kato got his start as a comic book professional being Terry Beatty's letterer and art assistant on Ms. Tree. Since then he's worked on various comic book titles such as Destroyer Duck, Thunderbunny, The Original Streetfighter and Elfquest Bedtime Stories. And, last but not least, he illustrates the current and ongoing comic book series Mr. Jigsaw, written by co-creator Ron Fortier. He's also illustrated children's books such as The Menehune of Naupaka Village, Jamie And The Fish-eyed Goggles, and the ongoing Barry Baskerville series. He does illustrations for Airship 27 Production.

KELLOGG, RICHARD L.
Born—20 May 1938
88 West University St.
Alfred, New York 14802
United States of America

E-mail: (rkellogg8@stny.rr.com)

Writer—Reviewer

Richard Kellogg is best known for his books and articles dealing with the exploits of the immortal Sherlock Holmes. His essays on the Great Detective have appeared in a variety of popular and professional publications. He has reviewed books in the mystery and science-fiction genres for Paperback Parade and New York Review of Science Fiction. Kellogg is the author of a popular series of mysteries for children which feature boy detective Barry Baskerville. Lavishly illustrated by noted artist Gary Kato, the stories introduce children to the legend of Sherlock Holmes while showing them how to develop their problem-solving skills. The most recent entry in the series is titled

"Barry Baskerville and the Buried Treasure" (Airship 27, 2019).

KLAUBA, DOUGLAS
Born—19 March 1963 543 Linden Rd.
Frankfort, Illinois 60423
United States of America

Website: www.douglasklauba.com E-mail: doug@douglasklauba.com
Artist—Teacher

Douglas Klauba has created cover artwork for books featuring such famous characters as *John Carter of Mars, Tarzan, Doc Savage, The Avenger, The Spider, Zorro, Kolchak: The Night Stalker,* and *The Phantom,* among others. In addition to his publishing work for companies including American Fantasy Press, Pegasus Books, Harper-Collins, Dynamite Entertainment, Image Comics, Radio Archives, Moonstone Books, and Edgar Rice Burroughs, Inc., Doug's paintings have been included in the art annuals of Spectrum: The Best in Contemporary Fantastic Art, the Society of Illustrators, and featured in Imagine FX magazine. His dramatic style, influenced in part by pulp magazine, golden age adventure illustration, and early movie poster art has earned him acclaim from collectors and clients around the world. His painting *Mercury Jack* was among the 250 works exhibited in the Spectrum Show at the Museum of American Illustration, his painting *Da Vinci's Dream* was awarded Best in Show at the 2005 World Fantasy Convention, and The Pulp Factory awarded Doug the Best Cover in 2020 for *Your's Truly, Johnny Dollar.* A poster of his painting *Stella 7* is hanging on Howard Wolowitz's bedroom wall on the hit television show Big Bang Theory, Season 5. When not teaching at the International School of Comics in Chicago, Doug is currently working on a creator owned illustrated pulp adventure, and *High Adventure: The Adventure Art of Douglas Klauba,* a collection of his pulp inspired paintings and illustrations.

KOHLER, CHRIS
Born—early 70s
Vancouver, WA
United States of America

website: www.relhok.com
E-mail: (chris@relhok.com)

Illustrator

Illustration contributor to three Airship 27 novels, as well as all nine Sentinels novels by Van Allen Plexico—and winner of the 2017 Pulp Factory Award for Best Interior Illustrations for book 8 of same. Also draws and letters occasional short comic book stories, and has worked on a couple of long form comic project collaborations such as The Season, and The Portland Underground.

LAI, RICK
Born—6 Oct 1955
3 Nicholas Ct
Bethpage, NY 11714
United States of America

website: www.amazon.com
E-mail: (rlai@optonline.net.net)

Writer—Editor - Reviewer

Rick Lai has written chronological studies of classic pulp heroes such as *Chronology of Shadows: A Timeline of The Shadow's Exploits* and *The Revised Complete Chronology of Bronze*. Rick's fiction about Victorian detectives and criminals has been collected in *Shadows of the Opera*, *Shadows of the Opera: Retribution in Blood* and *Sisters of the Shadows: The Cagliostro Curse*. As a homage to spaghetti westerns, Rick originated the Major Sabbath series published by Airship 27. He also regularly appears on the Lovecraft Ezine internet chats on Youtube. His article, "Poseidon and the God of the Robert E. Howard Universe," won the 2108 Hyrkanian Award from the Robert E. Howard Foundation.

LAMASTUS, JEREMY "J.L."
Born - 24, Sept 1972
5210 Stratford Rd
Evansville, IN 47710
United States of America

website - www.shadeofjeremy.com
E-mail: (sojdesigns@aol.com)
Twitter - @shadeofjeremy

Writer - Artist

Jeremy "J.L." LaMastus has been writing since he was a senior in high school. Around the first time he discovered Pulps as well. Reading Edgar Rice Burroughs' "Venus" novels loaned to him by a neighbor followed by his discovery of H. P. Lovecraft shortly there after. He has experimented with many styles of writing until he found Pulp writing to be the best fit. He mainly writes in the genres of Modern Adventure with his series "The Challenger Rangers" and Sword and Sorcery with "The Blue Dark." Both are available from Amazon. He is expanding with the addition of Crime Fighters which can be found through Airship 27, Space Opera and Weird Horror which he is currently working on his first stories in.

LAYNE, J. WALT
Born—22 Nov 1970
215 The Post Rd. Apt. J
Springfield, Ohio 45503
United States of America

website: https://jwaltlayne.wixsite.com/author
E-mail: (jwaltlayne@gmail.com)

Writer

Pulp writer best known for the Champion City series chronicling the rise of Detective Thurman Dicke for Pro Se Press. He has also penned short stories for a variety of Airship 27 anthologies including Tales From The Hanging Monkey Vol 2, Crimson Mask Vol 2, Secret Agent X Vol 5 and All American Sports Stories. Layne got his start writing for The Backwoodsman Magazine.

LEARY, ROMAN

Born - # June 1972
1750 Lizzard Slip Rd.
Washington, NC 27889
United States of America

E-mail: (romanleary@hotmail.com
Writer
Writer best known for authoring the first full-length novel in Ron Fortier's Brother Bones series, "Brother Bones: Six Days of the Dragon." Leary's work first appeared in the "Tales of the Shadowmen" anthology series from Blackcoat Press. His most notable work for Blackcoat was a series of stories featuring the Nyctalope, a controversial character from the classic era of French pulp fiction. His work has also appeared in "The Amazing Harry Houdini Volume 1" and "Masked Rider: Tales of the Wild West Volume 2", both published by Airship 27.

LEVINSON, LEN

Born—20 May 1935
Mount Morris, Illinois
United States of America

E-mail: (lenlevinson@icloud.com)

Writer

Author of 83 novels written originally under 22 pseudonyms, with an additional three novels under his real name for a total of 86. He created and wrote "The Apache Wars Saga" series by pseudonym Frank Burleson for Signet, "The Pecos Kid" series by Jack Bodine for Harper, the "The Rat Bastards" series by John Mackie for Jove, the "Searcher" series by Josh Edwards for Charter Diamond, and the "Sergeant" series by Gordon Davis for Zebra and Bantam, among other series and individual novels. Many have been republished as ebooks and in paper under his real name. He has been acclaimed a "Trash Genius" by "Paperback Fanatic" magazine, and was introduced as "a legend" at a panel during the 2017 Windy City Pulp and Paper Convention. His books have sold an estimated two-and-one-half million copies.

LIENHARD, SAMANTHA

Blossburg, PA 16912
United States of America
website: www.samanthalienhard.com

E-mail: (sam@samanthalienhard.com)

Writer

Horror, fantasy, and pulp writer Samantha Lienhard first found her writing niche with horror inspired by Ray Bradbury and H.P. Lovecraft. She received a B.A. in English from Mansfield University and an M.F.A. in Writing Popular Fiction from Seton Hill University, and has since published several short stories and novellas, including *The Book at Dernier* and *It Came Back.* In 2019, she entered the world of new pulp with her short story "The Domino Lady Takes the Case" and hopes to continue writing pulp fiction for many years to come. As a longtime gamer, she also writes scripts for video games and other types of interactive fiction.

LINDE, J.P.

Born—March 18, 1954
9155 Piccadilly Circle
Windsor, CA 95492
United States of America
website: www.jplinde.com

E-mail: jplinde@comcast.net

Writer—Screenwriter - Producer

Is the author and creator of the modern pulp novel, "Son of Ravage." For over thirty years, he performed stand-up comedy in clubs and colleges throughout the United States and Canada. In 1990 he made his national television debut on Showtime's "Comedy Club Network." He co-wrote the comedy musical "Wild Space A Go Go" (2010) and co-wrote and produced his first feature motion picture, "Axe to Grind" (2013). "The Holographic Detective Agency" is his first novel. A lifelong fan of the Doc Savage stories, it has always been his dream to bring a pulp hero to the modern age, telling it through the prism of modern pop culture while retaining the respect, adventure and wonderment so prevalent in the amazing writing style of the past.

LINES, STEVE
Born—20 Nov 1957
Calne, Wiltshire. SN11 0JX
United Kingdom

website: www.rainfallsite.com
E-mail: (rainfallrecords@doramail.com)

Artist—Editor—Musician—Songwriter—Writer

He is best known for running Rainfall Records & Books (with John B. Ford). Rainfall have published over 30 books, 20 records & CDs and over 300 chapbooks, many pulp related (such as *Strange Detective Stories*, *Tales of the Weird West*, *Lovecraft's Disciples*, *Swords of Adventure* and *Terror Tales*). Many of these feature Steve's artwork on the covers. He has illustrated books, chapbooks, fanzines and record/CD covers. He wrote *The Night Eternal* with John B. Ford and the pair has published a collection of short stories titled *Visions of Carcosa*. He has co-authored tales of *Varla of Valkarth* (set in Lin Carter's Lemuria) and the pulp adventure *The Moon the World Forgot* with Glen Usher. He has also pub-

lished *From Nightmares to Infinity* - a collection of his lyrics, two books on music - *Try Acid!* and *Mardenbeat* and three volumes of his musical autobiography - *From Nowhere to Obscurity*. He was the musical director of the *Strange Aeons* and *King in Yellow* CD albums and has performed and released music with his bands *Stormclouds*, *The Doctor's Pond* and *The Ungrateful Dead*. He continues to paint, write, record and perform - but not at the same time!

LOFFICIER, JEAN-MARC
Born—22 June 1954 1946
c/o Hollywood Comics
18321 Ventura Blvd., Suite 915
Tarzana, CA 91356
United States of America

website: www.lofficier.com
E-mail: (info@blackcoatpress.com)

Writer—Editor—Publisher—Translator

Often writing in tandem with his wife, Randy, Jean-Marc Lofficier has been a professional writer since 1979, first covering the Hollywood scene for a variety of American and foreign cinema magazines. They have edited and translated the award-winning Moebius graphic novels and other series, for which they won an Inkpot from Comicon in 1990. They have written numerous comic-books, sometimes in collaboration with Roy Thomas, Marv Wolfman and Len Wein, as well as a number of animation scripts including *Duck Tales* and *Real Ghostbusters*. They have authored a number of non-fiction books about science fiction and fantasy, including *The Doctor Who Programme Guide*. Their fiction includes ten novels, two collections of short stories, a children's novelization and over two dozen anthologies. They have also translated numerous French genre novels into English and in 2010 were awarded the French Grand Prix de l'Imaginaire. Jean-Marc is currently the editor-in-chief and main writer of Hexagon Comics and the publisher of two small press imprints, Black Coat Press in the USA and Rivière Blanche in France. Last year, he wrote a one-hour documentary on Stan Lee that aired on French network Canal-Plus.

LONER, BRIAN
Born - 12 Feb. 1976
Fort Collins, CO.
United States of America

website: brianlonerart.com
E-mail: brianlonerart@gmail.com
Instagram: @brianlonerart
Twitter: @brianlonerart

Artist

Interior illustrations in Marty Quade Private Detective Volume One—Airship 27 Productions. Illustrated and designer of World Prehistory Coloring Book - Kendall Hunt Publishing. Artist on Death Derby written by Ron Fortier (appearing in these anthologies; Ron Fortier's Tales of the Macabre and Todd Jones' Wicked Awesome Tales).

LOVATO, RAYMOND
Born - 31 Oct. 1950
41149 N. Sutter Lane
Anthem, AZ. 85086
United States of America

website - www.doc-atlas.com
E-mail: (raylovsue@aol.com)

Writer

Pulp writer best known for his continuing series DOC ATLAS; a homage to Doc Savage. Ray's literary aspirations began with being Associate Editor of his high school newspaper in Chicago. He continued as Associate Editor of the Saint Xavier University newspaper. His poetry was featured in the university literary magazine. Writing advertising copy was his next endeavor. This culminated in advertising director for the resort he built in Palm Springs, CA. His last few works of fiction for Airship 27 were contributions to "Sherlock Holmes, Consulting Detective." He is also known for elaborate and convoluted E-mail:s.

LOVISI, GARY
Brooklyn, NY

website: www.gryphonbooks.com
United States of America

Writer—Editor

Gary Lovisi is the author of various stories that have appeared in Airship27 books over the years, including such quintessential pulp characters as The Moon Man,

The Crimson Mask, The Purple Scar and The Phantom Detective. His latest books include The Secret Adventures of Sherlock Holmes: Book Three (Ramble House); and the forthcoming, Sherlock Holmes & Mr. Mac (Stark House Press, Black Gat Book #11); as well as his popular 2012 Holmes novel for Airship27, Sherlock Holmes: The Baron's Revenge. He is a Mystery Writers of America Edgar Nominated author for his Sherlock Holmes story, "The Adventure of the Missing Detective." Lovisi has also written three books in his Jon Kirk of Ares series, a sword and fantasy series inspired by Edgar Rice Burroughs' John Carter of Mars books; with two new books in the series: #4 The Mind Masters, and #5 The Time Masters, forthcoming this summer. You can visit him on Facebook.

LOWE, BRIAN K.
Born - July 24, 1956

website - http://www.brianklowe.word-press.com
E-mail: brianklowewriter@aol.com

Writer

A member of the Science Fiction and Fantasy Writers of America (SFWA) writing in genres all over the New Pulp map. His most recognized work is the time-travelling *Stolen Future* trilogy (*The Invisible City, The Secret City, The Cosmic City*), from Digital Science Fiction, featuring Captain Charles Clee, catapulted from 1916 France into the 863rd century, a world of reincarnated dinosaurs and uplifted species both friendly and hostile, suffering under the heel of alien invaders. A companion trilogy is in the works. Leaving science fiction for the hero pulps, he has penned three novels of the man known as Nemesis, from Digital Crime Fiction. An ex-spy investigates a terror plot to sabotage the 1932 Los Angeles Olympics, only to suffer apparently mortal wounds in a gun battle. From the ashes of his "death" arises Nemesis, the Man Without a Face, whose new identity in each book is a mystery not only to his enemies, but to the reader as well. Lowe has also produced stories of supernatural detectives, sword and sorcery, and superheroes for New Pulp venues such as Cirsova and StoryHack.

LOZITO, P.J.
New York
United States of America
Writer
Known for his vigilante character, the Silver Manticore. Upon publication, The Sting of The Silver Manticore rose to the top of Amazon's New Pulp bestseller list. That was followed by the single-author anthology, Silver Manticore: Friends and Foes. This collected previously published stories featuring a varied cast of his characters and anchored by a new Silver Manticore story, "The Death of the Silver Manticore." The story served as lead-in to the novel, Silver Manticore: Still at Large. He has also introduced the Revenant Detective in the e-book short, "Deadly Role." Due soon is the first Revenant Detective novel, tentatively titled Collision Course.

LYLE, JAMES E.
Born—10 October 1963
89 Walker Road
Waynesville, NC 28786
United States of America

Art by Morgan Fitzsimons

website: www.jameslyle.net
E-mail: (doodle@jameslyle.net)

Artist—Writer—Editor

Comics and pulps Artist (occasional writer and even more occasional editor) known for his interior illustrations for Domino Lady Volumes 1-3, Codename: Intrepid, Queen of Escapes (all from *Airship 27 Productions*), as well as on various comic book projects (SPARK, Hunters: Shadowlands, Grimm Fairy Tales, Tales From Neverland, Saint Germaine, DoorMan). Winner of 2018 Silver Reuben Award from the *National Cartoonists Society* in Advertising and Product Illustration for his work on Creepy Nature for the *Schiele Museum of Natural History*. Winner of the 2019 Golden Aster Award for Healthcare Education for his work on SPARK: Rising From The Ashes for *Centerstone Behavioral Health Services*.

MARTIN, C.E.
Born—November 1967
PO Box 542
New Albany, IN 47151 USA

website: www.Troglodad.com
E-mail: (Troglodad@gmail.com)

Writer

USAF veteran and retired criminal investigator, self-publishing men's adventure and new pulp since 2012, focusing on military, supernatural, and weird western topics in novels, short stories, and novellas. In 2019, began shifting his focus to non-fiction paranormal research and writing. In 2020 joined the independent podcasting community.

MAYNARD, WILLIAM PATRICK
Born—25 June 1971
Cleveland, OH
United States of America

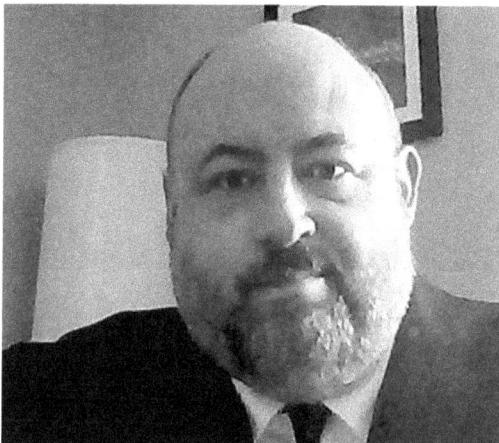

E-mail: (wpmaynard71@gmail.com)

Writer—Editor—Historian - Reviewer

Licensed continuation author for The Sax Rohmer Literary Estate. Author of novels and short fiction published by Titan Books, Black Coat Press, Bold Venture Press, Airship 27, Edge Publishing, and MX Books. Pulp historian with over 300 articles published by Black Gate, The Cimmerian, DMR Books, Altus Press, PulpFest, Blood 'n' Thunder, Windy City Pulp Stories, The Pulpster, and Van Helsing's Journal. Film historian contributing Blu-ray commentaries and supplemental materials to releases by MGM, Shout Factory, Kino Lorber, The Serial Squadron, and The Peter Sellers Appreciation Society.

An Executive Committee Member and Assistant Director of Marketing for PulpFest, Maynard also serves as an Editorial Board Member of The Battered Silicon Dispatch Box.

McCAULEY, TERRENCE
Born—1974
New York State
United States of America

website: www.terrencemccauley.com
E-mail: (terrence@terrencemccauley.com)

Writer

Terrence is the author of the award-winning Aaron Mackey westerns published by Pinnacle. He will also contribute three stand-alone novels to the successful Ralph Compton Series: THE KELLY TRAIL, RIDE THE HAMMER DOWN and an untitled novel published by Penguin. He is also the writer of the acclaimed University Series, which includes: THE FAIRFAX INCIDENT, A CONSPIRACY OF RAVENS, A MURDER OF CROWS and SYMPATHY FOR THE DEVIL, published by Polis Books. He has also written two award-winning pulp novels set in 1930 New York City—PROHIBITION and SLOW BURN. His World War I novella - THE DEVIL DOGS OF BELLEAU WOOD - won the Silver Medal for Historical Fiction from the Military Writers Society of America. His short story 'EL CAMBALACHE' was nominated for Best Short Story in the ITW's annual Thriller Awards. He has also had short stories featured in Thuglit, Spintetingler Magazine, Shotgun Honey, Big Pulp and other publications. He is a member of the New York City chapter of the Mystery Writers of America, the International Thriller Writers, the International Crime Writers Association, the Military Writers Society of America and the Western Writers of America. Terrence is an avid reader, a lover of classic movies and enjoys traveling. He's a huge cigar and soccer fan and supports Liverpool FC in the English Premier League and NYCFC in Major League Soccer. A proud native of The Bronx, NY, he is currently writing his next work of fiction.

McCORMAC, PHILIP
England

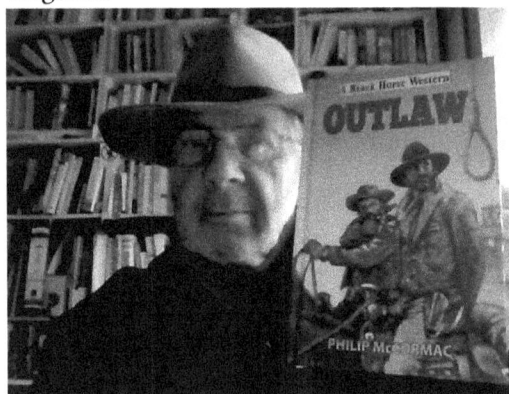

website: PhilipMcCormac.co.uk

Writer

Writes mainly westerns though on occasion has strayed into crime, fantasy and supernatural. Writes mainly for BLACK HORSE WESTERNS—twenty at the latest count. Another ten books published in in the above genres. Latest publication—EPITHAPH IN LEAD.

McFADDEN, HARDING
Born; 20 March, 1980
Quakertown, PA 18951
United States of America

website - www.facebook.com/profile.
php?id=100017549563192
E-mail: (munstermockingbird1313@hot-mail.com

Writer

Harding McFadden is a writer of YA science fiction adventure novels, and short fiction of all kinds. With Chester Haas, he is the writer of *The Children's War.* His solo work includes *The Great First Impressions Trip*, which one reviewer called "A must read for fans of libertarian sci-fi and fantasy," and the short story collection *The Judas Hymn.* His short fiction has been printed in Neo-Opsis Science Fiction Magazine, Lovecraft's Disciples, Strange Sorcery, and various anthologies, including *The Idolaters of Cthulhu, An Improbable Truth: The Paranormal Adventures of Sherlock Holmes*, and *Challenger Unbound.* He is currently at work on the next book in his YA series, along with whatever inklings of narrative ideas worm their way into his mind.

McNULTY, THOMAS
Born—18 Nov 1955

website: http://tommcnulty.blogspot.com
E-mail: (theregulators73@yahoo.cm

Writer—Reviewer

Writer best known for his biography of Errol Flynn and the New Pulp Westerns: Trail of the Burned Man, Wind Rider, Showdown at Snakebite Creek, Coffin for an Outlaw, The Gunsmoke Serenade and Ambush at Skyline Ranch. His New Pulp Sea Adventure story, The Adventures of Captain Graves, was published by Airship 27 and is available as an audio book from Radio Archives. McNulty hosts the YouTube channel program, McNulty's Book Corral, where he makes reading recommendations and insight into collecting rare and vintage books.

MENDENHALL, ROBERT J.
Born—1955
Southwestern Michigan
United States of America

website: www.RobertJMendenhall.com,
www.CodeNameIntrepid.com
E-mail: (Robert@RobertJMendenhall.
com)

Writer

Robert J. Mendenhall is the creator and author of the Code Name: Intrepid™ series of
pulp-adventure stories. *Intrepid* is a highly-
trained team of military and professional
civilians during the 1930s tasked by the
War Department to combat menaces to
the nation that are of unnatural or supernatural order. Their adventures have been
published by Chaosium Press, Kayelle
Press, Pro Se Productions, and Airship
27 Productions. Mendenhall is a retired
sergeant from a suburban police agency
near Chicago. He is also retired military
and a former Broadcast Journalist for the
American Forces Network, Europe. He is a
member of the Science Fiction and Fantasy
Writers of America, Mystery Writers
of America, International Association
of Media Tie-in Writers, and the Short
Mystery Fiction Society. Mendenhall
writes across genres including science fiction, horror, crime and suspense, and historical fiction. His work has appeared in
three Star Trek: Strange New Worlds anthologies published by Pocket Books, and
by Fey Publishing, Dark Quest Books,
Local Hero Press, Zimbell House Press,
Nomadic Delirium Press, Rogue Star
Press, Dark Alley Press, and the Saturday
Evening Post (.com).

MENGEL, BRAD
Ipswich QUEENSLAND
Australia

website: http://pulpybrad.blogspot.com
E-mail: (bunduki1975@live.com)

Writer—Editor—Reviewer

Paperback Fiction, the first major work on
the paperback heroes of the 70s, 80s such
as Brad Mengel is an Australian New Pulp
author. He is the author of *Serial Vigilantes
of* The Executioner and The Destroyer.
His fiction work includes new adventures
of Sherlock Holmes, Domino Lady and
Senorita Scorpion. He is the author of the
novel *Australis Incognito,* a new pulp novel
set in Australia with a team of multi-gen-
erational heroes.

MESSER, ADAM
United States of America

website: https://www.amazon.com/Adam-Messer/e/B07G72JS8P
Links to books, radio show, podcast, & social media: https://linktr.ee/adammesser
E-mail: adam.messer@gmail.com

Writer - Radio Show Host

Adam Messer is an author, journalist, and radio show host. He writes for the Savannah Morning News Do Savannah. The Adam Messer Show is live on Sundays from 3 - 5 pm EST. You can also listen to all of my shows on my podcast on Apple Podcasts and Libsyn. Adam Messer is a member of the Horror Writers of Association. He is the author of The Savannah Vampire Novel Series, as well as The Adventures of Tex Riddle, and The Cryline Wars. He started drawing as a kid, and is working on a graphic novel series, to be announced later. He loves connecting with other creators. If you are interested in doing an interview, please contact him at E-mail: listed.

MEYER, DREW
Lynchburg, VA
United States of America

E-mail: (drewmmeyer@hotmail.com)
Writer—Editor - Reviewer
Freelance genre/pulp writer and independent game designer. Included in 2015's *Legends of New Pulp Fiction* and the upcoming *Tales of Cape Noire*. Contributor to numerous anthologies. Publishers include: Airship 27, Who Dares Publishing, Watching Books, ATB Publishing, Chin Beard Books, Kozmic Press, Scaldcrow Games (Ron Fortier's Cape Noire sourcebook, Davey Beauchamp's Amazing Pulp Adventures, Rotwang City: City of Shadows, Bare Bones Beyond) In addition, is available as a Project Consultant. Samples available on request.

MILLER, CHUCK
Born—Oct. 12, 1963

401 12th Ave. S.E. Apt #188
Norman OK, 73071
United States of America

Blog - http://theblackcentipede.blogspot.com
E-mail: (drsivana99@gmail.com)

Writer

New Pulp/horror writer best known for his work on the Kolchak: The Night Stalker novel series from Moonstone Books. He also created and writes the Black Centipede series from Pro Se Press and the Bay Phantom series from Airship 27. He has also written novels and stories featuring Sherlock Holmes and the Avenger, and several short stories for horror anthologies. He holds a BA in creative writing from the University of South Alabama.

MILLER, PETER
Burbank, CA
United States of America

Writer—Film Editor

Peter Miller has three daughters and enjoys playing volleyball, board games and riding his sidecar motorcycle. He is currently working on his first novel.

MILLER, THOMAS KENT
Born—24 October 1945
Southern California
United States of America

website: www.thomaskentmiller.com
E-mail:thomaskentmiller@gmail.com

Writer—Editor - Reviewer

Thomas is known equally well in three totally different arenas. On one hand, he's written six H. Rider Haggard pastiches, all but one of which focus on Haggard's classic hunter-trader character Allan Quatermain. Three of these pastiches are novellas, two of which have been published in Airship 27's Publication's ALLAN QUATERMAIN: New Adventures. Four of these works also feature Sherlock Holmes. Thus, Thomas has some renown in both Quatermain and Holmes circles. In another arena, Thomas is known as an authority on nearly all Mars movies made since 1910 and has written the world's first movie- overview book entirely focused on Mars movies titled MARS IN THE MOVIES: A HISTORY, published by McFarland. In the third arena, he is considered an authority on the talented fin de siècle -era writer of horror tales Arthur Machen and has contributed several essays on Machen to UK literary journals. Indeed, one such essay was reprinted in 2019 in Hippocampus Press' prestigious The Secret Ceremonies: Critical Essays on Arthur Machen. Thomas has also provided US and UK literary journals with essays on Rider Haggard, M,R. James, David Lindsay, and the prolific pulp writer E. Hoffmann Price. In short, Thomas Kent Miller's spirit is clearly planted in the 1870s through the 1930s. This is made manifest by his intense interest in Victorian and Edwardian ghost stories, in the Hudson River School of landscape painting, and his two favorite authors, H. Rider Haggard and Arthur Machen. Yet his spirit also loiters on the planet Mars as imagined by the science fiction cinema of the 1950s and 60s. Finally, Thomas has created and curates a number of genre-related blogs and Facebook groups.

MILLHOUSE, CHARLES F.
Born—6 FEB 1965
17 JACOBS AVE
CHAUNCEY, OH 45719
United States of America

website: www.stormgatepress.com
E-mail: (stormgatepress@gmail.com)

Writer—Editor—Publisher

The author of twenty plus books in the Science Fiction—Fantasy—New Pulp genres. Millhouse published his first book "Keepers of the Past" in 1999, and his first New Pulp flavored book entitled: "In Memory Alone", the first of five in his Talon's Epic series in 2004. He created Stormgate Press in 2006 to further his publishing endeavors and in 2012 launched the first of his successful new pulp series, "The Captain Hawklin Adventures", in which he is best known, working with many talented cover artists, including Clayton Murwin and Marvel Comics Legend Sandy Plunkett. In 2021 he will edit and publish a New Pulp adventure magazine, entitled "Pulp Reality", focusing on some of the brightest New Pulp writers of the twenty-first century.

MINCEMEYER, DAMASCUS
Catawissa, Missouri
United States of America
Twitter—zombiestickman@gmail.com

Writer—Artist

Damascus Mincemeyer was exposed to the weird worlds of horror, science fiction and comics as a boy, and has been ruined ever since. He's now a writer and artist of various strangeness and has had short stories published in the anthologies Bikers Vs The Undead, Psycho Holiday, Monsters Vs Nazis, Mr Deadman Made Me Do It, Satan Is Your Friend, Monster Party, Wolfwinter (All from Deadman's Tome publishing, and books for which he also provided cover art), Fire: Demons, Dragons and Djinn, Earth: Giants, Golems and Gargoyles, Air: Slyphs, Spirits and Swan Maidens, Hear Me Roar (Tyche Books), Hell's Empire (Ulthar Press), Crash Code (Blood Bound Books), Appalachian Horror (Aphotic Realm), A Tree Lighting In Deathlehem (Grinning Skull Press), The Devil You Know (Critical Blast), On Time (Transmundane Press), the Sirens Call ezine, the Gallows Hill website, and the magazines Aphotic Realm and StoryHack.

MONNIN, M. A.
Born—1 July 1961

website: www.mamonnin.com
E-mail: (monninma@gmail.com)
Writer

M. A. Monnin's time-traveling trouble-shooter Hawk Hathaway made his debut in the short story "Siren Song," which appears in the Pro Se Production anthology *All That Weird Jazz*. Her other short crime fiction includes "Bad Ju-Ju" in Anthony-nominated *Malice Domestic 14: Mystery Most Edible*, and "St. Killian's Choice," a modern Cold War tale appearing in *Black Cat Mystery Magazine* No. 7. Her non-fiction endeavors include articles on Victorian literature, archaeology, gardening, and radio drama published in such diverse periodicals as *Nineteenth-Century Contexts*, *Texas Gardener*, and *Mystery Readers Journal*. A 2020-2021 board member of Mystery Writers of America-Midwest Chapter, M. A. continues to document Hawk Hathaway's cases from her home in Kansas City, Missouri.

MORRIS, BRIAN K.
Born—2 Mar 1956
1923 Charles Street
Lafayette, IN 47904
United States of America

Art by Steve Bryant

website: www.RisingTide.pub
E-mail: (bkmorris56@hotmail.com)

Writer—Editor—Publisher
Brian K. Morris has been a professional writer for over 20 years and a full-timer since 2012. A former playwright, he authored many pop culture articles that have appeared in BACK ISSUE Magazine, Hogan's Alley, RetroFan Magazine, and The Krypton Companion, among others too obscure to mention. He's also revived classic comic book characters such as Nature Boy, the Purple Claw, and the Original Skyman, all with a pulp-flavored sensibility. His parody/horror book Santastein: The Post-Holiday Prometheus has sold in North America as well as Great Britain, Germany, Japan, and China. In addition, his short stories have appeared in anthologies from Flinch! Books, InDELLible Books, Hailin Fine Art Publications, Lion's Share Press, GCD Publishing, NeoLeaf Press, and Cherry House Press. A former editor/writer for Chicago-based Silver Phoenix Entertainment, he scripts comic stories featuring real life Illusionist Master Ron Fitzgerald and Queen of the Paranormal Kadrolsha Ona Carole. Through his publishing company, Rising Tide Publications (formerly Freelance Words), he publishes a variety of books and comics including his own creations, Doc Saga and Vulcana. He's currently working on a Fantasy Romance novel, a new Vulcana novel, some new Captain Hawklin stories for Charles F. Millhouse's Stormgate Press as well as material for Pro Se Press and other publishers.

MOYERS, GENE
Born—1954
Resides in Beaverton, Oregon
United States of American

website: www.genemoyers.com
E-mail:contact page on my website

Writer

Best known as a New Pulp writer with many short stories, novellas and novels to his credit. Creator of "The Shrike," his female avenger and "The Dream Master," both original New Pulp heroes. Has written for several New Pulp publishers such as *Airship 27*, *Pro SE Press* and *Moonstone Books*. His short Story "Circle of Despair" published in *The Phantom Detective volume 1* by Airship 27 was nominated for a Pulp Factory Award.

He is also known for writing historic fiction and is the author of *GURPS: Crusades* published by Steve Jackson Games and is also the author of a series of alternate history stories set in his "Zeppelin World."

MUIR, SHANNON
Born—10 July 1972
PO Box 6385
Burbank, CA 91510
United States of America

website: www.mysteryshelf.com
E-mail:shannonmuirbooks@gmail.com

Writer

Wife of New Pulp Writer and Artist Kevin Paul Shaw Broden, also known for New Pulp stories she's written. Her best known is the digital single shot short story "Ghost of the Airwaves" released by Pro Se Press. She's also appeared in the anthologies EXPLORER PULP ("Hidden History"), NEWSHOUNDS ("Pretty as a Picture"), THE DAME DID IT ("Tragic Like a Torch Song"), and CRIME DOWN ISLAND ("Tropical Terror"), all released by Pro Se Press.

MULLANEY, JAMES
Massachusetts
United States of America

Writer

James Mullaney is a Shamus Award-nominated author of over 40 books, as well as comics, short stories, novellas, and screenplays. His work has been published by New American Library, Gold Eagle/Harlequin, Marvel Comics, Tor, Moonstone Books, and Bold Venture Press. He was ghostwriter and later credited writer of 26 novels in The Destroyer series, and wrote the series companion guide The Assassin's Handbook 2. He is currently the author of The Red Menace action series as well as the comic-fantasy Crag Banyon Mysteries detective series.

MURRAY, WILL
Born—28 April 1953
United States of America

website: www.adventuresinbronze.com
E-mail: (adventuresinbronze@gmail.com

Writer—Journalist - Editor—

Novelist, journalist and comics writer/editor is best known for his Wild Adventures series of novels, which revived Doc Savage, Tarzan of the Apes, King Kong, The Spider, John Carter of Mars and others. He ghosted the Destroyer paperback series for ten years, as well as individual novels starring The Executioner, Nick Fury and Mars Attacks. He won the Lamont Award in 1979 for his contributions to pulp history and in 2014 he won the Pulp Factory Award for Best Novel for *Doc Savage: Skull Island,* among other awards. He is the author of the non-fiction books, *The Duende History of The Shadow* and *Wordslingers: An Epitaph for the Western.* As a contributor to many prose anthologies, Murray has written short stories featuring a host of classic characters, including The Spider, Superman, Batman, Wonder Woman, Spider-Man, Ant-Man, the Hulk, Iron Man, the Gray Seal, the Green Hornet, The Secret 6, Sherlock Holmes, John Silence, Honey West, Zorro, Sky Captain, Cthulhu, Dr. Herbert West, Planet of the Apes and Lee Falk's the Phantom. Over the years, Will Murray edited the small press magazines *Duende* and *Skullduggery,* as well as serving as supervisory consultant for Radio Archives' Will Murray Pulp Classic line of ebooks and audiobooks. He worked as creative consultant and editorial supervisor for Odyssey Publications' line of classic pulp reprints during the 1970s and 80s. For nearly thirty years, Murray wrote for the Starlog Group of magazines, which included *Starlog, Fangoria* and *Comics Scene,* for which he covered the film, television and comic book industries. He also contributed heavily to various Lovecratian journals, ranging from *Lovecraft Studies* to *Crypt of Cthulhu.* With legendary comic book artist Steve Ditko, Murray created Marvel Comics' Unbeatable Squirrel Girl. He also scripted The Destroyer, The Punisher and Iron Man for Marvel.

MURWIN, CLAYTON DAVID
Born—4 July 1964
9541 103rd St. Apt 1222
Jacksonville, Fl 32210
United States of America

website: www.artoftheheromaker.com
E-mail: (cmerwin6@gmail.com)

Cover artist—Interior Illustrator Comics & Pulp

Comic and pulp artist who is best known for his work on the Charity Graphic Novels he produced and published through his Veterans Non Profit Heroes Fallen Studios Inc.org - Artist/Publisher/Editor for "Untold Stories From Iraq and Afghanistan Anthology" Volume 1 -Project Manager/Publisher/Artist for "KW60 Project" for the DOD Honoring those who fought in the Korean War. "Korean War "Volume 1 & 2 Graphic Novels. Cover Artist for Author Charles F. Millhouse's " Captain Hawklin and the Ghost Army " published b6 Stormgate Press. Interior Artist for "The Eye Of Dawn" by Author Brad Sinor published through Airship27 Publications.

NASH, BOBBY
Born—14 August 1971
PO Box 626
Bethlehem, GA 30620
United States of America

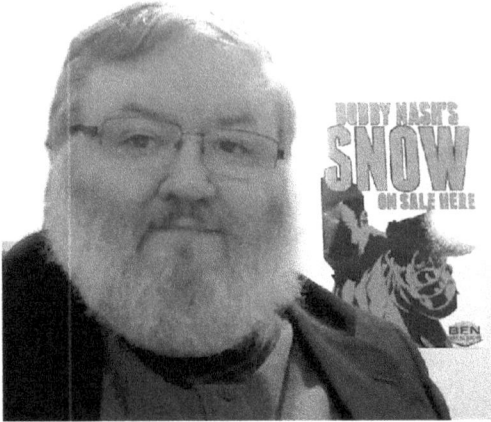

website – www.bobbynash.com
E-mail: (bobby@bobbynash.com)

Writer—Artist—Publisher

Bobby Nash is not a pulp hero, but he loves to write their adventures. Bobby is an award-winning author of novels (Snow Falls, Evil Ways, Deadly Games!, Nightveil: Crisis at the Crossroads of Infinity), comic books (Edgar Rice Burroughs' At The Earth's Core, Domino Lady, Operation: Silver Moon), short fiction (Domino Lady, Yours Truly Johnny Dollar, The Avenger), and the odd short screenplay (Starship Farragut "Conspiracy of Innocence, Hospital Ship Marie Curie "Under Fire"). Bobby is a member of the International Association of Media Tie-in Writers and International Thriller Writers. He occasionally appears in movies and TV shows, usually standing behind your favorite actor and sometimes they let him act. He can be seen in Creepshow, Joe Stryker, Doom Patrol, The Outsider, Ozark, Lodge 49, Slutty Teenage Bounty Hunters, and more. He also draws from time to time. For more information on Bobby Nash please visit him at www.bobbynash.com, www.ben-books. com, and across social media.

NEVINS, JESS
Born—30 July 1966
15607 Gilbertyn Dr.
Tomball, TX 77377
United States of America

website: www.jessnevins.com
E-mail: (jjnevins@ix.netcom.com)

Writer

Writer of nonfiction reference books who is best known for his *Encyclopedia of Fantastic Victoriana* (2015, 2020) and his annotations to Alan Moore & Kevin O'Neill's *The League of Extraordinary Gentlemen*. A college librarian by day, he has written a number of book chapters and book introductions. His books include *Horror Fiction in the 20th Century* (2020), *Horror Needs No Passport* (2018), *The Encyclopedia of Pulp Detectives* (2017), *The Encyclopedia of Pulp Cowboys* (2017), *The Encyclopedia of Pulp Adventurers* (2017), *The Encyclopedia of Fantastic Pulp Heroes* (2017), *The Evolution of the Costumed Avenger: The 4,000-Year History of the Superhero* (2017), and *The Victorian Bookshelf: An Introduction to 61 Essential Novels* (2016).

NOE, DAVID
Born- 14 Feb 1965
9000 NW 268th St.
Gower, MO 64454
United States of America

Facebook   Site-   https://www.facebook.

com/tradeofthetricks/
E-mail:- amazingthingspress3@gmail.
com

Writer- Editor- Publisher

Co-founder of InDELLible Comics and writer of several books including the Trade of the Tricks series and the pulp adventure books "Moon Man", "Fantastic 4N1", "The Alabaster Kid", and "The Wisdom of the Owl" among others. He has brought a mixture of Golden Age comics and Pulp adventures by mixing the public domain characters and creating new 'pulp' characters in the same world. InDELLible Comics primarily reinvents the public domain and orphaned characters from the defunct Dell Comics. Some of the company's full color oversized anthologies with card stock covers include All-New Popular Comics, Tales From the Tomb and House of Spades, with several others in the works.

NYE, CHRIS
Born—3 Nov 1965
12 Ravencrest Ct.
Columbia, SC 29680
United States of America

website: www.chrisnyeart.com
E-mail: (chrisdnye@comcast.net)

Artist - Writer

After years of working as an illustrator, writer and editor in the newspaper industry, got started in comics in 2004, creating the *Brother Destiny* character and series for Mecca Comics which was distributed by Diamond that year. During this time worked with comics veterans Dick Ayers, Al Milgrom and Greg Adams. Next worked with current Marvel Comics writer Chad Bowers on various projects from 2008-2010 — including the Bowers created characters *Doctor Impossible* and *Monster Plus*. In 2007-2010, did work for the online comics publisher, Flashback Universe, illustrating the *Prometheus* strip. Most recently completed illustration work for the Airship 27 Productions pulp novel *The Wraith*, a character created by Frank Dirscherl. Currently working with author Mark Ellis illustrating the *Lakota* graphic novel, originally penciled by comics veteran Jim Mooney. Future projects with Ellis are in the works. Also writing and drawing an update of *Brother Destiny* while considering various publishing routes for this new series.

ODOM, MEL
Born—15 Dec 1957
Moore, OK
United States of America

website: www.melodombooks.com
E-mail: (mel@melodom.net)

Writer—Teacher—Reviewer

Novelist best known for fantasy and science fiction, as well as tie-in novels for *Buffy the Vampire Slayer*, *The Executioner*, *Deathlands*, *Sabrina the Teenage Witch*, *Forgotten Realms*, *Shadowrun*, and other television, movie, and role-playing game properties. He's the co-creator of the action-adventure series Rogue Angel. His novel, *The Rover*, won an American Library Association Alex Award in 2002. His SF novel, *Lethal Interface*, was a Stephen Tall finalist. He has written Bass Reeves stories for Airship 27 Productions in the New Pulp line and has several other stories. He's the author of the forthcoming Rancho Diablo book series and writes in the Gunslinger series under the name A. W. Hart. *The Pecos Undertaker* is his first book in the Stark and Buchanan Western series about two young bounty hunters. He teaches in the Professional Writing program at the University of Oklahoma.

OLSEN, JOHN M.

Born—17 May 1963
6877 W Tracy Loop Rd
Herriman, UT 84096
United States of America

website: https://johnmolsen.blogspot.com/
E-mail: (JohnMOlsenWriting@gmail.com)

Writer - Editor

John M. Olsen edits and writes speculative fiction across multiple genres with a focus on stories about ordinary people stepping up to do extraordinary things. As the 2020-2021 President of the League of Utah Writers, he has encouraged and taught many fledgling writers. His short story "When Words Fail" won the 2018 DragonComet short story competition hosted by FyreCon, a conference dedicated to authors and artists. He edited the steampunk anthology "Put Your Shoulder to the Wheel" which won the League of Utah Writers Gold Quill award for collections in 2019.

OLSON, KEVIN NOEL

Born—3 December 1968
1859 Phillips Avenue
Butte, Montana 59701
United States of America

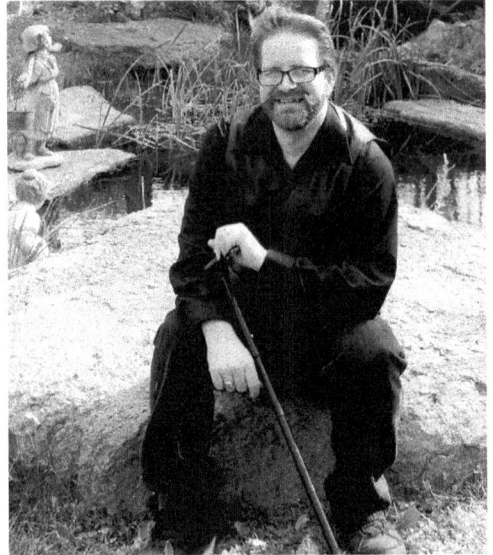

website: KevinNoelOlson.com
E-mail: (kno2skull@yahoo.com)

Writer—Publisher

Adventure author Kevin Noel Olson started publishing in 1995 with Secret Sanctum magazine. His adventure fiction works include Buk Bakus in 4891, Terror in Butte, The Coward, Springheeled Jack: Gunfighter, SHJ: Theatre of the Deranged, The Obscure, Entopia, novel for childen. The Eerey Tocsin trilogy is a series of YA novels. His anthology contributions include Secret Agent "X" #1, 2, 4, Green Lama, Semi Dual, Mystery Men & Women Vol. 3, Towers of Metropolis and Legends of New Pulp Fiction. The non-fiction novel, Terror in Butte. Mister Olson is currently working on non-fiction material set around Butte, Montana during the turn of the century.

OTIS, STEVE

Born—8 April 1963
1233, rue des Buissons
Neuville, QC G0A2R0
Canada

website: www.productionsmaeve.com
E-mail: (productionsmaeve@gmail.com)

Illustrator - Painter

Steve's started to draw at a very early age. Fueled by images of DC and Marvel comics. He soon discovered the great Warren magazines (Creepy and Eerie in the early 70's). From there he began to delve more deeply into horror, gothic and sci fi type art. Heavily influenced by Frazetta, Boris and Richard Corben, he began experimenting in oil paints in 1988. His first desire was to become a fantasy illustrator and did quite a bit of work in that style in the late 90's for CCG (collectible card games). By the early 2000's, he gave up on oil painting as it was way too time consuming and started using exclusively acrylics. He began to look for techniques to challenge his artistic style in a more "Fine Art" vein while keeping a firm thematic of dark art. He had grown tired of the generic sword and sorcery genre. He began working with more textures, abstract approaches and has been working in this vein ever since.

PANUSH, MICHAEL

Born—2 Oct 1989
2623 Independence Avenue.
West Sacramento, CA 95691
United States of America

website: michaelpanush.com
E-mail: (m.panush@yahoo.com)
Writer
Michael Panush has distinguished himself as one of Sacramento's most promising young writers.His books with Curiosity Quills include *The Stein and Candle Detective Agency, Volume 1: American Nightmares, Volume 2: Cold Wars*, and *Volume 3: Red Reunion*, all featuring a pair of occult detectives in the 1950s, *Dinosaur Jazz*— where *The Great Gatsby* meets *Jurassic Park* — a story about a Lost World battling against the forces of modernization; *El Mosaico, Volume 1: Scarred Souls, Volume 2: The Road to Hellfire*, and *El Mosaico, Volume 3: Hellfire*, a Western about a bounty hunter whose body was assembled from the remains of dead Civil War soldiers and brought to life by mad science; and Dead Man's Drive, a 1950s urban fantasy about a hot rod-riding zombie. With Airship 27, he created the Clay Shamus—a story of a golem detective. His short fiction has been published in Towers of Metropolis and George Chance: The Green Ghost from Airship 27. His most recent novel from Pro Se Press, *Ape's Honor, a novel of Victoria's Ape*, tells the tale of an intelligent noble gorilla in an alternate 1880s London.

PARENTE, AUDREY

Born—3 Jan 1948
2726 NW 104th Ave.
Sunrise, FL 33322
United States of America

Art by Steve Lines

website: www.boldventurepress.com
E-mail: (editor@boldventurepress.com)

Writer—Editor

Audrey began writing stories, freelance newspaper articles and collecting pulp fiction magazines in the mid-1980s. Her biography of pulp fiction author Hugh Cave was published in 1988. She completed Ted Roscoe's bio in 1992 and began work on Judson P. Philips' life story. A journalism career went into high gear at The Daytona-Beach News Journal from 1992 thru 2012, when she took early retirement. Her return to the pulp world took her to Pulp AdventureCon in 2012 and led to joining Rich Harvey in Bold Venture Press and eventually completing Judson P. Philips' biography.

Author: *Audrey's Private Haunts* (Miskatonic University Press 1987); *Pulpman's Odyssey: The Hugh B. Cave Story; Pulpmaster* (Starmont House 1988): *The Theodore Roscoe Story; Once a Pulpman* (Starmont House 1992); *On Any Dark and Spooky Night* (Ormond Beach Observer 1992); *Pulp Noir* (Bold Venture Press 2015); *The Secret Life of Judson P. Philips as Hugh Pentecost* (Bold Venture Press 2016); numerous fanzines — see: http://www.philsp.com/homeville/FMI/d/d4299.htm#A152319.

Editor at Bold Venture Press: *Pulp Jazz: The Charles Boeckman Story; Where Memory Hides* by Richard Lupoff; *Timely Confidential: When the Golden Age of Comics was Young* by Allen Bellman; *Zorro: The Daring Escapades; Pulp Adventures* (quarterly from #15 forward); SPWAO (Small Press Artists and Writers Organization) president, treasurer and newsletter editor, various years mid-1980s-early 1990s)

PEEL, JOHN

Born - January 24th, 1954 86 Ozone Street Manorville, NY 11949

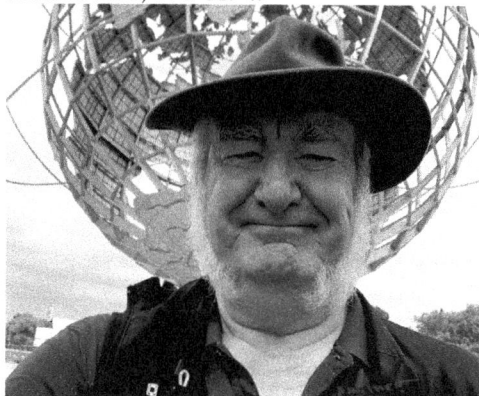

E-mail: johnpeel@optonline.net
Facebook: Facebook.com/JohnPeelAuthor
Writer

John Peel was born in England but moved to the U.S. in 1981. He began writing articles for magazines in 1980, and edited "Fantasy Empire" for several years. He's written over a hundred novels. These include creating his own fantasy series ("Diadem" and "Dragonhome"), and a large number of TV tie-in novels for shows like "Doctor Who", "Star Trek", and "The Outer Limits". He's also written about two dozen short stories, which are being collected into two volumes later this year.

PHILLIPS, GARY
Born — 24 August 1955
Los Angeles, CA

website: https://gdphillips.com
E-mail: — gdogg855@aol.com

Writer—Editor

He was weaned on the images of Kirby and Kane in comics and too many re-runs of the original *Twilight Zone*. In addition to writing the adventures of the Green Hornet and Kato, Kolchak the Night Stalker, the Avenger, Operator 5, Johnny Dollar, and the Spider for Moonstone, Phillips created Jimmie Flint, Secret Agent X-11. This was for a linked anthology he edited entitled *Day of the Destroyers*. He also co-edited the *44 Caliber Funk* anthology featuring his nod to '70s men's adventure paperback characters, Booker Essex, the Silencer. Also for Moonstone he wrote the cool *Danger A-Go-Go* graphic novel teaming up Captain Action, freelance spy Derek Flint and private eye Honey West. For Pro Se Productions, Phillips conceived, co-edited and contributed to *Black Pulp* I & II featuring his character Decimator Smith in 1930s Los Angeles, as well as stories for *Asian Pulp* and the *Adventures of the Bronze Buckaroo*. Additionally for that outfit, he took his modern-day hawkshaw Nate Hollis, begun as a comics miniseries for DC/Vertigo, and transported him to prose in stories by Phillips and other writers in and out of new pulp in *Hollis P.I.* and *Hollis for Hire*. He also contributed a story to Airship 27's first of several anthologies about legendary lawman Bass Reeves, and with his sometimes writing buddy Christa Faust, co-wrote a prose adaptation of the classic Batman vs. Joker graphic novel *The Killing Joke*. (Sketch by Phil Parks)

PITTS, JIM
Born - 19th JAN 1950
Blackburn. Lancashire. England
United Kingdom

E-mail: (jimpittspitts@Hotmail.com)

Artist

Jim Pitts started submitting B&W pen and ink art work in 1970. First to the fanzines, David Suttons SHADOW, and Jon Harveys BALTHUS. He immediately won his first award with the Ken McKintire statuette for that years best artist at Novacon 1971. Jim later was awarded the British Fantasy Society awards for best artist in the years 1992 & 1993. The move from b&w to colour work evolved and he did covers for Fantasy Tales and Kadath, amongst others. His work can be found on, and in, publications from the U.S.A, UK and EUROPE , such as Nyctalops, Etchings & Odysses, Whispers, W.Paul Ganleys Press, Fedogan & Bremer, Pegana Press and many others. Amongst the authors Jim has illustrated many stories for is Adrian Cole, and he has recently completed the pictures for a collection of Adrian's ELAK Of ATLANTIS stories due from PULP HERO PRESS this year. Jim continues to work in the Fantasy and Horror genre, and also counts to his credit, a collection of his work published in 2017 by Parallel Universe Publications entitled: THE FANTASTICAL ART OF JIM PITTS: ROLLING BACK THE YEARS. Jim is currently at work on a project for Centipede Press to be published in 2021 and some other pieces for Phantasmagoria Magazine in Northern Ireland.

PLEXICO, VAN ALLEN
Born - 1968
Smithton, IL 62285
United States of America

website - www.plexico.net
E-mail: (vplexico@gmail.com)

Writer - Editor - Publisher

Writer/editor who is best known for the Sentinels superhero novel series, he also writes crime fiction (Vegas Heist) and Military SF/Space Opera (Lucian; the Shattering series), as well as writing, creating and editing numerous anthologies and nonfiction works for many different publishers (Blackthorn; Gideon Cain; Mars McCoy; Assembled! Vols 1 and 2). A three-time winner of "Best Novel of the Year" from the Pulp Factory Awards, he also won "Best Anthology" for the Last of the Mohicans story collection he edited. He is the publisher of White Rocket Books and the host of the White Rocket Podcast.

PORTER, ALAN J.
Born—13 Oct. 1959
Pflugerville, TX
United States of America

website: http://alanjporter.com
Twitter—(@alanjporter
E-mail: alan@alanjporter.com

Writer

Alan J. Porter writes about stuff, and makes-up stories too. Pop Culture, Comics, High-Adventure fiction, Movies, and more. He has written adventures featuring classic characters such as Sherlock Holmes, Allan Quatermain, Houdini, The Musketeers, will Bill Hickok, and private eye Rick Ruby; as well as his own New Pulp adventurers, The Raven and The Lotus Ronin. His pop-culture non-fiction work has featured properties such as Batman, Star Trek, The Beatles, G.I. Joe, Battlestar Galactica, and James Bond. He has also written comics for Tokyopop, BOOM Studios, Marvel, Disney.

POWELL, MARTIN

https://www.facebook.com/martin.powell1
http://www.amazon.com/Martin-Powell/e/B001JRXRSU

Writer

Martin Powell has written many of the most popular characters in the industry, including Superman, Batman, Popeye the Sailor, and Tarzan of the Apes, in comics and in prose, for Disney, Marvel, DC, Dark Horse, among many others. Nominated for the prestigious Eisner Award for his work with Sherlock Holmes, he is also the creator of The Halloween Legion, a nominee for the Stan Lee Excelsior Award, and his Tall Tale of Paul Bunyan won the coveted Moonbeam Golden Award for Best Children's Graphic Novel. As the author of almost a dozen different ERB online comics series, and the critically acclaimed Jungle Tales of Tarzan graphic novel published by Dark Horse, Powell has written more Edgar Rice Burroughs characters than any other contemporary writer. In 2017, he received the coveted Golden Lion Award for his on-going contributions to the legacy of Edgar Rice Burroughs. His newest children's books, Private Eye Princess and the Emerald Pea and Rapunzel vs. Frankenstein, twist familiar fairy tales into original adventures for 21st Century readers.

POWERS, AARON
Born—21 Jan 1985
Loveland, CO

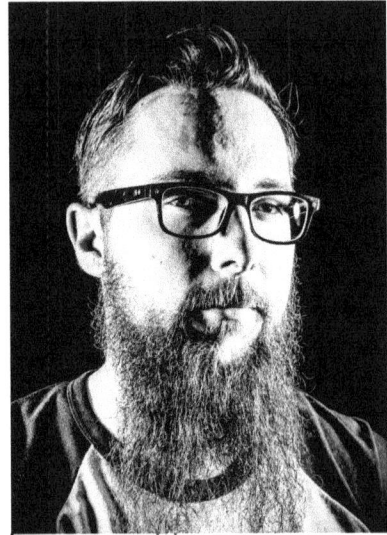

website: www.writingpowers.com
E-mail: (drifter.poet@gmail.com)

Writer

Aaron Powers was born and raised in central Nebraska. He received his Bachelor's degree in English: Writing and Literature from Wayne State College in Wayne, NE in 2007. From 2007 to 2010, Aaron and his wife lived in Massachusetts, where he worked as a design and editorial assistant in Boston. After moving to Loveland, CO, Aaron worked as a freelance writer and editor, and published his first novel, *Children of Light: Book One: The Silver-Haired Boy*, in 2014. His first published comic book story was featured in *Front Range Tales, Volume 1* from Redbud Studio in 2018. His short story "The Mask of Mesud" will appear in an upcoming Dan Fowler G-Man anthology from Airship 27 Productions. Aaron is employed as a Lead Content Marketing Specialist at Madwire, a marketing and design company in Fort Collins, CO, where he has worked since 2014. He is currently writing new short stories, comic book scripts, and the next installment of his *Children of Light* series.

POWERS, LAURIE
Born—25 Aug 1957
United States of American

Facebook: facebook.com/daisybaconau-thorizedpage

E-mail: (lauriepowers12@gmail.com)

Writer—Historian

Laurie Powers is the granddaughter of author Paul S. Powers (1905-1971), who contributed over 450 stories for *Wild West Weekly, Weird Tales, Western Story, Thrilling Western, Popular Western,* among others. Instrumental in getting her grandfather's memoir, *Pulp Writer: Twenty Years in the American Grub Street,* published by University of Nebraska Press in 2007, and wrote the prologue and epilogue included in the book. Over the next several years she and Altus Press published two more anthologies of her grandfather's works. In 2011 she began researching the life of Daisy Bacon, editor of Street & Smith's *Love Story Magazine,* and in 2019 her biography of Bacon, *Queen of the Pulps: The Reign of Daisy Bacon and Love Story Magazine,* was published by McFarland Books. *Queen of the Pulps* was nominated for a PCA/ACA award as well as noted as a noteworthy book in the *Washington Post* in 2020. Contributed articles to various publications, wrote the introduction to the new edition of Bacon's 1954 book *Love Story Writer,* (Bold Venture Press, 2016) and was a contributor to *The Art of the Pulps: An Illustrated History* (Ellis, Hulse, et al.; IDW, 2017). In 2016, she was awarded the Munsey Award for her contributions to the study of pulp fiction.

PURCELL, DARRYLE
Born—14 June 1947
P.O. Box 20072
Bullhead City, ZA 86439
United States of America

website: amazon.com/author/darrylepurcell

E-mail: (purcells@citlink.net)

Writer—Cartoonist
Darryle Purcell currently writes and illustrates the Hollywood Cowboy Detectives adventure series as well as the Man of the Mist neo-pulp books. He spent a lot of years as a cartoonist, most notably in layout and character design for television animation in the early 1970s, illustrator and art director for educational comic books in the mid '70s, and newspaper editorial cartoonist in the '80s. He also spent several years as managing editor of a daily newspaper and, later, as a government public information director. During his newspaper years, Purcell garnered many local and statewide honors for his political cartoons, editorials and columns. His Man of the Mist and Hollywood Cowboy Detective books, available in Kindle and paperback editions, not only embrace the illustration style of pulp publications of the 1930s, they also honor the pulse-pounding cliffhanger action of the Saturday matinee serials of

the same era. Purcell, a Vietnam veteran, also writes short stories, including "Jungle Rot," a wartime mystery first published in *Heater* mystery magazine.

RAMOS, JAMIE
Born—16 Dec. 1967
St. Louis, MO
United States of America
E-mail: (jaimeramos5150@yahoo.com

Writer—Editor

Writer of short stories and assistant editor. Most notable: creator and editor of the award-winning anthology, Singularity: Rise of the Posthumans (published by Pro Se Productions.) Co-creator and assistant editor of the anthology, Legends of New Pulp (published by Airship 27.) Jaime often proofreads manuscripts for Airship 27 and is working on his debut novel.

RANDISI, ROBERT J.
Born: 8 AUG 1951
3665 S. Needles Hwy, apt. 7G
Laughlin, NV 89029
United States of America

E-mail: RRandisi@sbcglobal.net

Writer –Editor—Reviewer—Publisher – Founder

Booklist has said he may be "the last of the pulp writers." He is the author of over 600 books, editor of 40 anthologies, co-founder of Mystery Scene Magazine, The American Crime Writers League, and Western Fictioneers - founder of The Private Eye Writers of America, creator of The Shamus Awartd, co-creator of The Peacemaker Award. He has received the 2013 Readwest President's Award— The Life Achievement Award from The Private Eye Writers of America—The Life Achievement Award from The Western Fictioneers—The Life Achievement Award from The Short Mystery Fiction Society.- The John Seigenthaler Humanitarian Award from Killer Nashville. For 7 years he was the mystery reviewer for The Orlando Sentinal. He has had a book published every month since January 1982, and has been published in 6 decades.

RAWDING, CHRIS
Born—1 Mar 1968
Taunton, MA
United States of America

website: www.rawding.daportfolio.com
E-mail: (rawddesign@yahoo.com)

Artist

An eminent artist, educator and out-
door enthusiast. A keen artist from his
early days living on the South Shore of
Massachusetts where he currently resides
with his two sons.

After attending the Museum School of
Fine Arts and receiving his Bachelor's in
Commercial Illustration from the Art
Institute of Boston, specializes in digital
Illustration, conceptual design & book il-
lustration. As an eclectic visionary with a
gallery including; pop culture, steampunk
chicks, superhero and famous phantoms.

RAYMER, HERICKA R.
Born - 26 February 1974
P.O. Box 307
Moscow, Tennessee 38057
United States of America

website - herikarraymer.webs.com
E-mail: (herikarraymer@gmail.com)

Writer - Editor

Herika R. Raymer grew up consuming
books - first by eating them, later by reading them. Her parents instilled a value of
focus and hard work while encouraging
a creative spirit; prompting her to dabble
for over 30 years. Since 2009, her short
works have appeared in Dark Oak Press
and Media, Falstaff Books, Pro Se Presents,
and Seventh Star Press among others.
She has edited single-works like Kill Me
When You Can and anthologies including
Idolators of Cthulu. Mrs. Raymer is mar-
ried to a devoted man, adores two wonderful children, and spoils a spastic dog in
West Tennessee, USA.

REASONER, JAMES
Born—5 June 1953
Azle, Texas
United States of America

website: www.jamesreasoner.com
E-mail: (james53@flash.net)

Writer—Editor—Publisher - Reviewer

A professional writer for more than 40
years, James Reasoner has written close
to 400 novels in a variety of genres, under his own name and many pseudonyms.
He has also written more than 100 shorter
pieces of fiction, including a New Pulp story featuring the classic character Richard
Henry Benson, The Avenger. "Death in
Clown Alley" appeared in THE AVENGER
CHRONICLES, published by Moonstone
Books in 2008. He has also written sto-

Art by Morgan Fitzsimons

ries featuring The Green Hornet ("The Cold Cash Kill", THE GREEN HORNET CHRONICLES, Moonstone Books, 2010) and The Lone Ranger ("Hell on the Border", THE LONE RANGER CHRONICLES, Moonstone Books, 2014). Writing under the name Jackson Cole, he is the author of the Jim Hatfield novella LONE STAR FURY (Rough Edges Press, 2015), featuring the lead character from the long-running Western pulp TEXAS RANGERS. In addition, he writes and publishes the popular Rough Edges blog (https://jamesreasoner. blogspot.com) which regularly features reviews of pulp novels and stories, both old and new, and is the owner and moderator of the WesternPulps E-mail— group (https://groups.io/g/WesternPulps), where the members have been discussing Western pulps, their authors, and their characters since 1999.

REINAGEL, WAYNE
Born—7 May 1961
410 South Morrison
Collinsville, IL 62234
United States of America

website: www.pulpheroesmorethanmortal. webs.com
E-mail: (reinagel@aol.com)

Writer—Editor—Publisher - Illustrator
Pulp adventure writer/artist/publisher is best known for his Pulp Heroes trilogy (More Than Mortal, Khan Dynasty, and Sanctuary Falls.) Pulp Heroes - Sanctuary Falls won the Pulp Factory Award for Best Novel of 2017. His other novels include The Inner World Adventure, The Hunter Island Adventure, The Cast Away, and a steampunk adventure Modern Marvels - Viktoriana. All of theses titles are published under the banner of Knightraven Studios and features covers and interior artwork by the author.

RIETHMEIER, RAY Born—28 March 1971 12015 Townview Road Minnetonka, MN 55343 United States of America

E-mail:ray@PULPlications.com Editor
As an editor, proofreader, and copyeditor, Ray Riethmeier is a nitpicker for fun and profit. Although he has worked for the last quarter century as an attorney and editor of law books, he derives his greatest satisfaction from editing New Pulp and pulp fiction reprints for Altus Press, Steeger Books, Meteor House, PULPlications, and Airship27, among others. Ray has a particular interest in Sherlock Holmes, and he has lent his talents to numerous publications for BSI Press, Rosemill House, and the Norwegian Explorers of Minnesota (his local Baker Street Irregulars scion society). If he has his way, Ray will be superamalgamated.

RESTRICK, JASON
Born—11 May 1985
Maple Ridge
British Columbia
Canada

Writer

Jason Restrick writes in various genres but favours horror and fantasy most of all. His first story, "Robert's Refuge," appeared in the Nov/Dec 2008 issue of *The Willows*, a charming and hauntingly assembled black-and-white magazine that was devoted to gothic weird fiction. His early stories were published under the byline J.R. Restrick. He discontinued the initials in 2018 with the publication of "The Temple of Baktaar" in Bryce Beattie's magazine *StoryHack Action & Adventure*. The sequel, "Beyond the Temple of Baktaar," appeared in issue 4 in 2019. Jason's work has also appeared in *Weird Tales*, *Heroic Fantasy Quarterly*, *Bête Noire*, and *Helios Quarterly Magazine*. He is glad to be a part of the pulp writing community as it continues the old campfire tradition of sharing wonderful, unique, and often strange stories from familiar and emerging voices.

RICCI, ROBERT
Born—1963
Hyde Park, MA
United States of America
E-mail: (robertmricci@hotmail.com)

Writer—Editor
Robert has written tales for several books published by Airship 27 Productions, featuring classic pulp icons the Phantom Detective and Domino Lady, as well as his own creations, Rutherford Jones and Solution Sparks.

RITZLIN, D.M.
Born—24 January 1980

website: www.dmrbooks.com
E-mail: dmr@dmrbooks.com

Writer—Editor—Publisher

Ritzlin runs DMR Books, a publishing house specializing in sword-and-sorcery fiction. His adventures in the new pulp field began in 2015 with the release of the first of three *Swords of Steel* anthologies (which included stories by Howie K. Bentley and Byron A. Roberts, among others). Later he branched out into reprinting classic material by authors such as Robert E. Howard, Henry Kuttner, Manly Wade Wellman, Poul Anderson, Nictzin Dyalhis, and more. His own stories, which are influenced by Clark Ashton Smith, Jack Vance, and Fritz Leiber, have been published in *Cirsova Magazine* and the anthology *Flashing Swords 6* (edited by Robert M. Price). A collection of his short stories is tentatively scheduled for release in the fall of 2020. DMR Books has built a dedicated following based on Ritzlin's vision of sword-and-sorcery: uncompromising fiction packaged with incredible cover art.

ROBERTS, BYRON A.

Born—17 Oct 1970
Sheffield, Yorkshire, United Kingdom

website: www.byron-a-roberts.co.uk
E-mail: (official_bal-sagoth@hotmail.co.uk)

Writer

Byron Roberts is a writer of pulp sword & sorcery stories and also the vocalist, lyricist and founder of the UK extreme metal band Bal-Sagoth. An English Literature graduate, Roberts conceived Bal-Sagoth as a symphonic black metal project built upon an elaborate fantasy and sci-fi oriented lyrical concept, inspired by the literature he grew up with, particularly the classic pulp stories of Robert E. Howard and H.P. Lovecraft. The lyrical mythos of his Bal-Sagoth universe goes far beyond the band's six album discography, encompassing novels, novellas and short stories. Among Byron's published works are "The Voyages of Caleb Blackthorne" trilogy (comprising "Into the Dawn of Storms",

"A Voyage on Benighted Seas" and "The Scion at the Gate of Eternity") appearing in the "Swords of Steel" paperback series from DMR Books, the novel "The Chronicles of Caylen-Tor" published by DMR Books, the short story "Chronicles of the Obsidian Crown" appearing in the anthology "Barbarian Crowns" published by Barbwire Butterfly Books/Horrified Press, the short story "Darkfall: Return of the Vampyre Hunter" appearing in the anthology "Devil's Armory" published by Barbwire Butterfly Books/Horrified Press, the poem "When Dead Cthulhu Dreams" appearing in the anthology "Beyond the Cosmic Veil" published by Barbwire Butterfly Books/Horrified Press, the short story "Caylen-Tor" appearing in the anthology "Dreams of Fire and Steel" published by Nocturnicorn Books, the poem "The Hallowing of the Wolf-King" appearing in The Hyborian Gazette published by Carnelian Press, and the collaborative novel "Karnov: Phantom-Clad Rider of the Cosmic Ice" published by DMR Books.

ROBERTS, ERWIN K.

Born—Early 1947
8505 East 95th Terrace
Kansas City, Missouri 64134
United States of America

website: https://erwin-k-roberts.com/
E-mail: erwin.k.roberts@gmail.com

Writer— Art Creator

Erwin K. Roberts is a pen-name for a fellow accidentally born with one that became a U.S. political household name. He grew up in a late TV adopter family, so, in addition to books and comics, he listened to the radio versions of The Lone Ranger, Sgt. Preston, Sky King, Space Patrol, and others. Erwin always wanted to be a creator in some media. He began submitting stories to professional magazines while serving with the U.S. Army in Korea, in 1972. In 1979 Erwin wrote a novel in an attempt to crack the second wave of the "Let's clone Mack Bolan." market. No luck there, either. From about 1980 to 1997 all of Erwin's creative energies went into producing and appearing on Kansas City's Public Access cable TV station. He interviewed everyone from R.Lee Ermey and Chuck Norris to Larry Niven and both John Romita's. Not to mention Ice-T and a couple of Klingons. At the beginning of the new Century Erwin began writing again. First for Tom and Ginger Johnson's *Fading Shadows* imprint. Then over 25,000 words for an online roleplaying game for a year. In 2005 Erwin discovered the electronic version of self-publishing. He published *Plutonium Nightmare*, the 1979 novel mentioned previously. That, and some mutual friends from the roleplaying game, helped get him started with New Pulp publisher Airship-27. Erwin has contributed to eight Airship-27 books. He has appeared in six titles from Pro Se Publications, and one from Mechanoid Press. Erwin self published two volumes about The Voice from his own Modern Knights Press. More will follow...

ROSS, JOHN BEAR Born—July 1975 4860 W. Charleston Park Ave.
Pahrump, NV 89048 United States of America Website: bearross.com
E-mail: (johnbearross@gmail.com)

Writer

His short stories have appeared in Airship 27 anthologies for Secret Agent X and Mars McCoy. His ongoing Junctionworld science fiction series has earned International Best Seller status on Amazon Kindle.

RUSSELL, ERNEST
Born—22 MAY 1963
4520 S Sherwood Forest Ste 104-124
Baton Rouge, LA 70816
United States of America

website: https://ernestrussell.com/
E-mail:: erussell1313@hotmail.com

Writer—Editor—Publisher—Reviewer

Ernest Russell has written for Pro Se Productions, Beyond the Threshold Studios, and the literary journal Violet Windows. Some of his favorite things (besides coffee) are Science Fiction, Horror, Steampunk, and Fantasy books and movies. His writing splits among those genres. When not creating, Ernest is a freelance editor, look for him on Reedsy.com. He was a Content and Copy editor for 'Tales of The Interstellar Bartenders Guild' winner of the 2019 Pulp Factory Award for Best New Pulp Anthology. On his blog you'll find a mix of his writing, promotion and reviews. As often as possible, you can find him playing board games or an RPG. In the last year, Ernest has joined the staff at Pro Se as submissions editor and, as time allows, content and copy editor.

RUSSETTE, C. WILLIAM
Born—30 Dec 1972
Williamsport, PA 1770
United States of America

website: https://www.face-
book.com/Artist-C-William-
Russette-1655154048053701
E-mail: (cwilliamrussette@gmail.com)

Writer—Artist

C. William Russette is a writer of both short and long fiction. He has written comics for Modern Pulp Comics and Airship 27 Productions. His short stories have appeared in anthologies for Airship 27, Pro Se Productions and Emby Press. His debut novel SHAMANSKIN was released through Pro Se Productions. THE CRIMSON MASK anthology through Airship 27 was nominated for the Best Pulp Revival in the New Pulp Awards. He lives in Pennsylvania with his wife, son and two golden retrievers.

SALMON, ANDREW
Born—28 Feb 1966
301-116 East 16th Ave.
Vancouver, BC V5T 2T2
Canada

website: https://www.amazon.com/
Andrew-Salmon/e/B002NS5KR0
E-mail: (andrewsalmon2000@yahoo.com)

Writer—Publisher—Reviewer

Historical adventure and pulp writer best known for his Sherlock Holmes tales. His Fight Card Sherlock Holmes boxing tales for Fight Card Books broke new Sherlockian ground. He won the Pulp Factory Award for Best Pulp Short Story of 2009 for "The Adventure of the Locked Room," which first appeared in Sherlock Holmes Consulting Detective Vol. 1 from Airship 27 and in 2014 for "The Adventure of the Limehouse Werewolf," from the anthology Sherlock Holmes Consulting Detective Vol. 4. His novel, The Light of Men, was added to the Holocaust Memorial Museum Library in Washington, DC as well as earning recognition from the 761st Tank Battalion. He writes the continuing adventures of his own character, Eby Stokes, which are published through Timepiece Press. He also writes the Berlin Noir Review blog.

SAUNDERS, CHARLES
Born—12 July 1946
Nova Scotia
Canada
Writer—Editor - Screenwriter
Charles R. Saunders is an African-American author and journalist. During his long career, he has written everything from novels both fiction and non-fiction, to screenplays and radio plays. Inspired in Africa, he created the fictional continent Nyumbani (which means "home" in Swahili), where the stories of Imaro, his sword and sorcery series, take place. Publisher Donald A. Wolheim suggested that Saunders turn his Imaro stories into a novel. Six of the early novellas would later be used in his first novel, *Imaro*, which was published by Daw in 1981. Saunders lives in Nova Scotia. He works the night shift there at a local newspaper as a copy editor. Saunders has written four non-fiction

books about the Nova Scotia black community, including a collection of his columns. In 2006, small press Night Shade Books made a deal with Saunders to publish an updated edition of *Imaro*. In 2008 the second novel in the updated Imaro trilogy *The Quest for Cush* was published by Night Shade Books. He released *Dossouye* through Sword & Soul Media. Dossouye herself is a woman warrior inspired by the real-life female warriors of the West African Kingdom of Dahomey. Her first stories appeared in Jessica Amanda Salmon's *Amazons!* and Marion Zimmer Bradley's *Sword and Sorceress,* two anthologies designed to increase the number and recognition of female heroes in sword and sorcery fiction.

SAYELL, TIMOTHY A.
Born-5 Sep 1974
Las Vegas, NV

website- https://theadventuresite.blogspot.com/
E-mail: (theadventuresite@yahoo.com)

Writer-Artist

A lifelong lover of cliffhanger serials, old time radio, silver and golden comics and the pulp heroes who proceeded them, he is best known for his serial "The Adventures of Bradley Brackett" from Abandoned Towers Magazine and its audio version on the "Beam Me Up Podcast". His stories have appeared in small press magazines and ezines including Raygun Revival, Flashing Swords, and Big Pulp Magazine. Currently, he is composing a series of novellas for the Kindle, starting with his post-apocalyptic science fantasy, Mutant World.

SEQUEIRA, CHRISTOPHER
Born—More than 21 Years Ago
9 Weldon Street
Burwood, NSW, 2134
AUSTRALIA

website: https://www.facebook.com/christopher.sequeira.5
E-mail: chrissequeira@optusnet.com.au

Writer—Editor—Publisher

Comics and short story writer, anthologist/ editor and sometime publisher; has written for Marvel, DC, Boom Studios, with most distinctly pulp connections being works relating to the "Justice, Inc." franchise (short story for Moonstone Books; two-part comic-book story co-written with Mark Waid for Dynamite), or for Cthulhu-mythos fiction; however, also an internationally-known essayist, comic-scripter, short story writer, anthologist and editor on Sherlock Holmes-related material; his long-delayed, licensed Dr Fu Manchu anti-racist revival comic-book series with frequent collaborator Wai Chew ('Chewie') Chan is finally due 2021. (Photo by Sarah Barker.)

SHAW, ADAM B.
Born - 16 Jan 1973
Unites States of America

Art by Mo Jackson

website www.abshaw.com
E-mail: (adambenetshaw@gmail.com)

Artist

Adam B. Shaw's painted art can be seen on multiple covers for Airship 27 Productions including Jim Anthony vs. Mastermind, Sinbad: The New Voyages vol 6, The Wraith, Sun Koh: Heir to Atlantis, Comanche Blood, Sherlock Holmes: Consulting Detective 9, The Bay Phantom and many others. Work for New Pulp and Pro Se includes Johnny Dollar, Silver Manticore, Asian Pulp and the Black Pulp series. Adam's comic book work includes Harpe: America's First Serial Killers, Memphis Noir for Akashic Books and Bloodstream, which he created and wrote with his wife Penelope, for Image comics. Shaw studied painting at the Cleveland Institute of Art in Ohio and at the Edinburgh College of Art in Scotland. He has shown his oil paintings and drawings in group and solo shows in museums and galleries all over the US and in England. Shaw has also worked on several murals for historical museums, illustrations for role-playing games, storyboards for film and stage set design.

SIMPSON, HOWARD
Born—10 June
Los Angeles, CA 90017
United States of America

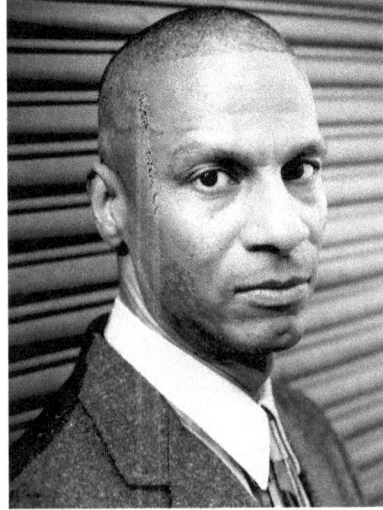

website: http://abbadabba.com/
E-mail:jobz@abbadabba.com

Artist - Writer

He was born in Newark, NJ. His mom says he started drawing when he was two years old. After finding some old, discarded comic books in the basement, he decided he would become a storyteller. His passion is for helping people tell their stories, as well as his creations. He attended Arts High School in Newark, NJ. Afterward, he received his BFA from Temple University's Tyler School of Art. Currently, living in Los Angeles, CA doing storyboards, animation, and comics. His clients include Warner Bros. Animation, Disney, DC Comics, Simon & Schuster, Random House, HBO, and various advertising agencies. He is creating his webcomics on Tapas at https://tapas.io/abbastudios You may see his work online at http://abbadabba.com/ and get social with him on Instagram @abbastudios
Check out his blog on creating comic books, strips and graphic novels at Just Create https://www.justcreate.net/ I am the winner of the 2020 Pulp Factory Award for BEST PULP INTERIOR ILLUSTRATIONS - Bulldog Drummond: On Poisoned Ground—published by Airship 27.

SINOR, BRADLEY H.
Born—Oct. 13, 1952
Tulsa, OK 74105
United States of America

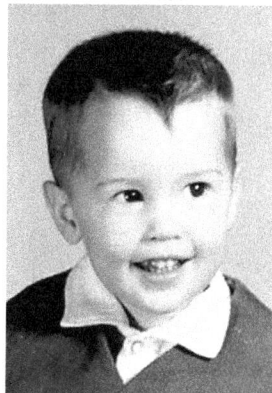

website: https://sinor.osfw.online/
E-mail:: sinor13@yahoo.com

Writer—Reviewer

This Science Fiction, Fantasy and Horror writer is best known for his short stories and interviews of Genre notables. He was a preliminary nominee for the 2000 Nebula Award for his short story Dreams And Nightmares. He is a former newspaper reporter and local book reviewer. His titles include novels—THE HUNT FOR THE RED CARDINAL, published by Eric Flint's Ring Of Fire Press, and THE EYE OF DAWN, published by Airship 27. His collections include: WHERE THE SHADOWS BEGAN, ECHOES FROM THE DARKNESS, DARK AND STORMY NIGHTS, IN THE SHADOWS and OF TWO MINDS: LOCATION SHOOT, IT'S A MIRACLE AND OTHER STRANGE STORIES.

SIPPO, ARTHUR C.
Born—30 Jan 1953
300 Brentmoor Court
Highland, IL 62249
United States of America

website: http://artsreviews.libsyn.com

E-mail: (artsippo@aol.com)

Writer—Reviewer—Podcaster

Art has been a fan of Adventure Fiction, SciFi, Comics, since 1958 when his beloved Aunt Helen bought him a copy of the reimagined Flash superhero comic. He expanded his reading into more substantive books on classic speculative fiction by HG Wells, Jules Verne, Jack London, Arthur Conan Doyle, Olaf Stapledon, Isaac Asimov, Arthur C. Clarke, H. P. Lovecraft and Robert Heinlein. But he became most enamored with the Pulp fiction of the 1930s and 1940s when Aunt Helen introduced him to the Doc Savage reprints in the 1960s. From there he began reading The Shadow, The Avenger, Conan, and Tarzan among many others. He has written several articles and stories over the years but is best known for his reimagining of the German Pulp character Sun Koh. He also hosts the Art's Reviews Podcast interviewing authors and publishers of Pulp and adventure novels.

SKINNER, DAVID
Born—16 Feb 1963
Michigan
United States of America

website: www.davidskinner.biz
Twitter—@SpawnOfMars

Writer

Always on the shoreline of science fiction

(swimming in the lake or camping in the forest nearby). In the 1990s, contributed to the literature of juvenile fantasy, having three books published by Simon & Schuster: the novels *You Must Kiss a Whale* and *The Wrecker*, and the collection *Thundershine: Tales of Metakids*. Also contributed to the collection *Trapped!*, edited by Lois Duncan. Wandered for many years afterward. Did create and publish *The Giant's Walk* (a wondrous novel in which an astronaut seeks the miraculous intervention of a beatified priest, who, a century before, had pursued a Giant to Mars). Was energized by the Pulp Revolution and the call to heroic and superversive fiction. As of 2020, was published twice by StoryHack Magazine, twice by Stupefying Stories, and once by Cirsova Magazine. Also contributed to the collections *PulpRev Sampler* and *Planetary: Pluto*. Creator of Hamlin Becker & Anya Day. Looking forward to years of making weird and adventurous tales.

SLEMONS, JEFF
Born - November 5th 1965
Greeley, CO 80634
United States of America

Website – www.jeffslemons.com
www.comicartfans.com
E-mail (jeff@jeffslemons.com)

Artist

Jeff has been an illustrator for just over 30 years. He has done a variety of comic book and graphic novel projects for multiple clients. Some are in the traditional pen and ink format and others are fully painted comics. He has worked with Kingstone Publishing on a variety of their Bible graphic novels. Other projects include Mark Ellis' sci-fi space drama "Deathhawk", and several story projects for PKMM Entertainment, CARtoons Magazine as well as a handful of other clients who's books you have never heard of. All artwork for these projects can be found at Comic Art Fans. A variety of commissioned pieces can be seen there as well. Jeff loves comic books. He loves creating them even more.

SMITH, COPPER
Born — 3 Dec 1967
3441 Dupont Ave South #103
Minneapolis, MN 55408
United States of America

website - https://coppersmithcom.wordpress.com/
E-mail:: copperwright@gmail.com

Writer/voice actor/audio drama producer

Copper Smith has littered the online world with new pulp tales of suspense, danger and bad decisions. His written work has been featured in Pulp Modern, a Twist of Noir, Exquisite Corpse 2, Near to the Knuckle, Shotgun Honey and Beat to a Pulp. Additionally, his pulpy audio drama has been featured on such podcasts as Tales to Terrify, Ragged Foils, Crime City Central and Thrills and Mystery Podcast. His Jake Legato PI series is available on Amazon.

SMITH, DAVID C.
Born August 10, 1952
Lives in Palatine, Illinois
United States of America

website: http://blog.davidcsmith.net/
E-mail: daves1952@att.net

Writer - Editor

Fantasy author best known for his sword-and-sorcery fiction, particularly his continuing series of novels and short stories featuring the character Oron and his collaborations with Richard L. Tierney for the Red Sonja series of novels in the 1980s. He is also the author of the respected fantasy trilogy *The Fall of the First World* as well as the recent mainstream novels *Dark Muse* and *Bright Star*. Smith won the 2018 Atlantean Award from the Robert E. Howard Foundation for *Robert E. Howard: A Literary Biography* as Outstanding Achievement, Book. Now retired after a nearly 30-year career as a medical editor, Smith works part time as a freelance editor, continues to write fiction and articles, and spends quality time with his wife, Janine, and his daughter, Lily.

SPENCER, MATT
Born—11 May 1979

website: https://mattspencerauthor.word-press.com/
E-mail: (msdragonwolf@gmail.com)

Writer—Reviewer

Matt Spencer has been a boxer, bouncer, journalist, radio DJ, Renaissance Faire performer, actor, factory worker, restaurant cook, and a no-good ramblin' bum. His short fiction has appeared in *Aphelion, Broadswords & Blasters, EconoClash Review, StoryHack Action & Adventure, Red Sun Magazine*, and *Weirdbook*. He's the acclaimed author of the Deschembine Trilogy (*The Night and the Land, The Trail of the Beast,* and *The Blazing Chief*), as well as *Changing of the Guards* and *The Renegade God*.

SPURLOCK, DUANE
Born—24 Jan 1959
Louisville, KY
United States of America

website: https://pulprack.blogspot.com/

E-mail: (pulprack@gmail.com)

Writer—Reviewer

Writer in various new pulp genres, best known for his collaboration with Jim Beard on the novel *Airship Hunters*. He's written short stories in the western, science fiction, and adventure categories, including two stories featuring public domain jungle hero Ki-Gor (in *Jungle Tales: Volume 1* and *Ki-Gor: Jungle Lord*) and stories about a 1970s-era masked Mexican wrestler (El Tigre Azul) who fights supernatural and human monsters (*Three Witches*). He introduced Shalimar Bang, a contemporary consulting detective, in "The Dream Stalker." A historical adventure novelette, "Fighting Alaska," featuring Wyatt Earp, Tex Rickard, and Rex Beach, was published as part of the Fight Card series. He also illustrated *The Bleeding Horse and Other Ghost Stories* by Brian J. Showers, which won the 2008 Children of the Night Award from The Dracula Society.

STAHLBERG, LANCE
Born—1970
Chicago, Il.
United States of America

website - LRStahlberg.com
E-mail:Contact from Website

Writer

Born in Chicago, raised on a healthy diet of superheroes, sci-fi, fantasy, anime, James Bond, Mack Bolan, revenge flicks, gangster movies, and all things military from GI JOE to Hurt Locker. He debuted in comics as a founding member of the Shooting Star Comics posse and self-published under the label Rogue Wolf Entertainment. He has also adapted classic adventures like Moby Dick and the Three Musketeers into graphic novels. The genre defying author turned his focus to prose in 2014, when he was nominated for Best New Writer by the New Pulp Awards. He has contributed novellas to Super Powered Fiction, Pro-Se Press, and Airship 27, and writes the Marc Rinaldi Thrillers and other series under the pen name L.R. Stahlberg. He currently hails from Outer Chicagoland with his wife and stepson.

STARR, RICHARD DEAN
Born—6 Mar 1968
Chatsworth, CA 91311
United States of America

website: www.RichardDeanStarr.com
E-mail: (rdeanstarr@gmail.com)

Writer—Editor—Screenwriter

Author, editor, and screenwriter best known for credits in books, comics, magazines, and newspapers, as well as credits on multiple produced feature films. He began publishing professionally in a Los Angeles trade newspaper at the age of sixteen, and over the next thirty years, wrote or edited more than 200 articles, columns, stories, books, comics, screenplays, and graphic novels. At the age of twenty-one, Starr was a reporter and Entertainment Editor for the former *Southeast Georgian*® and *Camden County Tribune*® newspapers (now the *Tribune-Georgian*®), and was one of the youngest Active Members in the 120-year history of the Georgia Press Association. Licensed media tie-in characters Starr has written for include Hellboy, Zorro, The Green Hornet, Sherlock Holmes, The Lone Ranger, The Avenger, and Kolchak: The Night Stalker, among others. Starr served as co-editor of the Moonstone Books® Captain Action® comics line with Matthew Baugh and the crime anthology *Sex, Lies, and Private Eyes*, with Joe Gentile. Starr co-authored "Unnaturally Normal," a *Kolchak: The Night Stalker®* and *Dan Shamble, Zombie P.I. ®* comic team-up, with *New York Times* bestselling *Star Wars®* and *X-Files®* author Kevin J. Anderson. Their original script was later published in a signed, limited edition by Gauntlet Press. As an industry-leading feature film screenwriter and script consultant, Starr has contributed to produced motion pictures starring actors including Zack Galifianakis, Malcolm McDowell, Tom Sizemore, Amber Tamblyn, Haley Joel Osment, Costas Mandylor, Robert Culp, Bryan Batt, and Richmond Arquette. He is a member — or former member — of the Horror Writers Association (HWA), the Science Fiction and Fantasy Writers of America (SFWA), the International Association of Media Tie-In Writers (IAMTW), and the International Thriller Writers (ITW). He has been a judge for both the ITW "Thriller" awards and the IAMTW Scribe Awards.

STIEGLITZ, JOAB

Born—30 Dec 1965
7122 Vantage Drive
Alexandria, VA 22306
United States of America

website: www.joab.stieglitz.com

E-mail: (joab.stieglitz@gmail.com)

Author—Publisher - Game Master

Author of the Utgarda and Thule trilogies of supernatural thriller novels set in the 1920s and 1930s. Best known for The Old Man's Request: Book One of the Utgarda Trilogy. He is also author of The Lush of Liechtenstein, the first fluff piece for the Venus 1888 miniatures and role-playing game. Also publisher at Rantings of a Wandering Mind. Stieglitz is a software application consultant by day, and also a professional online role-playing game master with Zero Session.

SUBRAMANIAN, SCREENIVASAN
Tamil Nadu
INDIA.

Writer

S. Subramanian is a retired professor of economics who, after his superannuation, has found it possible to indulge an old fascination of his for stories of shots in the dark and screams in the night. He has written several Sherlock Holmes pastiches which have been published in David Marcum's edited anthologies for MX Books, Airship 27's *Sherlock Holmes: Consulting Detective* series, *Sherlock Holmes Mystery Magazine*, and *Mystery Weekly Magazine*, apart from other pieces in outlets such as *Weirdbook* and *Mystery Readers Journal*.

SWEET, JONATHAN (JAY)
Born—17 Oct. 1976
2398 Molnau Court
Chaska, MN 55318
United States of America

website – www.brickpicklemedia.com
E-mail: (jsweet@brickpickle.com)

Writer—Editor—Publisher - Reviewer

Award-winning journalist and editor; author of six books, including one pulp collection featuring his character The Red

Art by Steve Bryant

Jackal, and two non-fiction pulp guides, both of which were Amazon No. 1 New Releases. As the owner of Brick Pickle Media, a Minnesota-based communications firm and publisher, he publishes pulp collections under the Brick Pickle Pulp imprint. He has also served as an editor for multiple pulp publishers, working on dozens of books. He is the host of the weekly Pulp Nostalgia Audiocast, which features recordings of classic pulp stories and pulp-inspired Old Time Radio episodes.

TAYLOR, SEAN

Born—2 May 1968
572 Leaflet Ives. Tr.
Lawrenceville, GA 30045
United States of America

website: www.thetaylorverse.com
E-mail: (staylor104@aol.com

Writer—Editor
Sean Taylor is an award-winning writer of stories. He grew up telling lies, and he got pretty good at it, so now he writes them into full-blown adventures for comic books, graphic novels, magazines, book anthologies and novels. He makes stuff up for money, and he writes it down for fun. He's best known for his work on the best-selling Gene Simmons Dominatrix comic book series from IDW Publishing and Simmons Comics Group (which one reviewer called "the pulpiest pulp on the stands"). He has also written comics for TV properties such as the top-rated Oxygen Network series The Bad Girls Club. His forays into new pulp include the award-winning P.I. Rick Ruby of The Ruby Files Volume 1 and Volume 2 (2013 Pulp Ark winner for Best New Character, co-created with Bobby Nash) and characters ranging from the Black Bat and the Phantom Detective to the Golden Amazon and Secret Agent X. In 2012, he tied with fellow pulpster Chuck Miller for the Best New Writer category of the Pulp Ark Awards. In the 2018 Pulp Ark Awards, The Ruby Files Volume 2 took home the award for Best Anthology (along with Best Interior Art and Best Short Story). His fiction has been published by Penguin Books, IDW Publishing, Moonstone Books, Airship 27, Pro Se Press, and others, and he has explored such realms as steampunk, horror, pulp, young adult, fantasy, superheroes, sci-fi, and even samurai frogs on horseback (seriously, don't laugh). However, his favorite contribution to the world will be as the writer/editor who invented the genre and coined the term "Hookerpunk." He maintains a writers blog for writing instruction and writer promotion at www.badgirls-goodguys.com.

VANCE, MICHAEL Born—18 July 1950

1427 S. Delaware Ave.
Tulsa OK 74104 United States of America

E-mail:: MiklVance@Yahoo.com
Writer—Comics   Historian—Journalist—

Reviewer

He has written for magazines in seven countries and as a columnist and cartoonist in over 500 newspapers. His history book, "Forbidden Adventure: The History of the American Comics Group", has been called a "benchmark…" His credits include the comic strip, Alley Oop, and wrote his own strip, Holiday Out, that was reprinted as a comic book. Vance also wrote and created several original comic books. His work has appeared in multiple comic book anthologies and he is listed in two reference books, the "Who's Who of American Comic Books" and "Comic Book Superstars". His short stories have been published in many publications and most were recorded by legendary actor William Windom. One was nominated for the international 2004 SLF Fountain Award for Best Short Story. The first pulp book in his horror trilogy, "Weird Horror Tales", from Airship 27 has favorably been compared to Lovecraft and Bradbury. The second book is "Weird Horror: The Feasting; the final is "Weird Horror Tales: Light's End". The same publisher has released "Young Nemo and Black Knights", "Motor City Manhunt", "Sslits" and "Snake: Nest of Vipers". He also co-wrote the satiric novel, "Global Star" and the suspense thriller, "The Equation". His first Christian book was "The Thief of Two Worlds", which was followed by. "All In Color for a Time" and, "Klockwerks". Vance's weekly column, Suspended Animation, was published for twenty years and read by approximately 4,000,000 readers a year. It is the longest, continuously published comics review column in the world. He created the Oklahoma Cartoonists Collection and was a keynote speaker at the "Uncanny Adventures of Okie Cartoonists" exhibit at the Oklahoma Historical Museum in Oklahoma City.

VANN, MARK ALLEN
Born—29 Jun 1968
De Pere, WI

website: www.xepicopress.com
E-mail: (kgrroth@hotmail.com)

Writer—Publisher

A fresh, if somewhat weathered face in New Pulp, Mark was the founder of True Metal Lives where he worked with hundreds of underground bands worldwide, producing several music compilations and writing hundreds of album reviews. His first pulp release "Eight Against The Darkness" came out in 2020 under Xepico Press. Two more books are currently in the works.

VAUGHN, SCOTT P, 'Doc'
Born—Aug. 3rd 1975
4634 W Cavalier Dr.
Glendale, AZ 85301
United States of America

website: www.vaughn-media.com

E-mail:: mnvwho@gmail.com

Artist—Writer—Publisher

Scott P. 'Doc' Vaughn is an illustrator and writer living in the Phoenix area since 1990, hailing originally from Milwaukee, Wisconsin where he was raised with an encouraged imagination. He has tuned those imaginings into zines (M&V), websites, webcomics (such as Warbirds of Mars), print comics, and novels, as well as hundreds of personal and freelance illustrations. He has been published online and in select books and periodicals. He also co-edited (with Kane Gilmour) and contributed two short stories to his own 2014 New Pulp Awards-nominated anthology, Warbirds of Mars: Stories of the Fight! Among Scott's interests are classic illustrations and movie genres, vintage, and a severe predilection for 'Doctor Who'. His work takes many nods from pop, pulp, and classical culture from the early 20th century through today.

WALKER, JOSH
Born—6 July 1984
2200 Park Pl.
Cheyenne, WY 82001
United States of America

website: www.joshwalkerbooks.com
E-mail: (sharkwalker@ gmail.com

Writer—Editor—Publisher
Fantasy writer is best known for his international best selling Luke Coles books, an Urban Fantasy four book series. He has worked writing stories for various video games, including Phoenix Dawn and the Rise of the Witch. He is the Manager and owner of Forgotten Places Publishing, has worked as freelance editor on countless novels, and ghost written over ten novels. He continues to write fantasy novels and short stories as well as autobiographical books, chronicling his time as a missionary in Chile and as a pizza delivery driver.

WATSON, I.A.
Yorkshire, England

website: http://www.chillwater.org.uk/writing/iawatsonhome.htm
E-mail:ia_Watson@zoho.com

Writer

I.A. WATSON started out as a pinch-hitter short story writer filling in at the last minute when a Sherlock Holmes tale was needed quickly. His body of work now includes fifteen novels, five collections of short stories, and a volume of feature articles, in addition to contributions to over forty multi-author anthologies. Most of his stories are also available in e-book and audiobook format. They feature well known characters such as Sherlock Holmes, Robin Hood, Bulldog Drummond, Harry Houdini, Hercules, St George, and Sinbad the Sailor, along with original creations such as Sir Mumphrey Wilton, the Transdimensional Transport Company, and Vinnie de Soth, Jobbing Occultist. Watson has turned his hand to many kinds of genre fiction, often with "work to order" commissions which keep him sharp and pay some bills. He is a columnist and public speaker as well as a cloistered garret-dwelling writer. He likes to combine his loves of mythology and history with mystery and humour and is known as a man who can never avoid adding in a footnote. He cites his influences as J.R.R. Tolkein, Stan Lee, George MacDonald Fraser, and Dorothy L. Sayers. Watson's work has been recognized with three Pulp Factory Awards for Best Short Story - "The Last Deposit" in *Sherlock Holmes Consulting Detective* volume 2 (2011, Airship 27), "The Fort of Skulls" in *Pride of the Mohicans* (2014, White Rocket) and "The Death of Robin Hood" in *The Legend of Robin Hood* (2019, Airship 27) - with nine other shortlisted nominations for Best Short Story and Best Novel, and a 2013 Pulp Ark award for Best Author.

WELCH, GERALD
Born—September 10, 1964

website: www.jerrywelch.com
E-mail: (jerry@jerrywelch.com)

Writer—Artist—Publisher—Designer
Jerry is a lover of art in all its forms, whether it be visual art, books or music. He is best known as co-author of the *Legacy* novels with the late Warren Murphy (*currently writing the eighth book in the series The Homecoming*), but also authors his own series, *The Last Witness (currently at book six).* Jerry provides artwork for both series and designs all promotional goods. He also produced an over-sized hardback collector omnibus for both series. Each book is over four hundred pages and contains a detailed encyclopedia with character entries, maps

and other behind the scenes bonuses. He was an early leader in digital art and became the lead artist for the Seoul Summer Olympics. He won a Thomas Jefferson award for directing and multiple other awards for directing and editing and is one of only three people to be named an honorary Master of Sinanju. He was co-awarded the *Al Hartley award* for Best *Comic* Book for his entry in the "MEGA-UNITY Seven Day Challenge". Jerry served in the United States Army as a Broadcast Journalist (*Good Morning Vietnam! but on the television side of things*) and ran for the US House of Representatives in 1996. In other creative areas, Jerry has invented three board games (*DOMINION: Four player chess—TRIBUTE: The Sinanju board game and the upcoming HOMESTEAD*), two custom guitar designs (*IMPERIUM and STRATOSPHERIUS*) and is working on his second album and a community app.

WHALEN, JOHN
Springfield, VA
United States of America
Blog—www.johnwhalen.wordpress.com
E-mail: (whalen@cox.net)

Writer—Publisher—Reviewer

Neo-Pulp writer in a variety of genres. Best known for his Weird Western novel "Vampire Siege at Rio Muerto" and short story collection "Hunting Monsters is My Business, the Mordecai Slate Stories." He's also written the Spacewestern novel, "The Big Shutdown," and the Space Noir short story collection, "This Ray Gun for Hire and other Tales." His most recent release is the acclaimed sword and sorcery epic "Tragon of Ramura." He's published a number of other short stories in various anthologies, most of which can be found on his Amazon author page at: https://www.amazon.com/John-M.-Whalen/e/B003XVAG0M/ref=ntt_dp_epwbk_0. Whalen also reviews movies on DVD and Blu-Ray for www.CinemaRetro.com, and blogs on various topics at www.johnmwhalen.wordpress.com.

WHEATLEY, MARK
Born—27 May 1954
Insight Studios
PO Box 685
Westminster, MD 21158
United States of America

website: www.MarkWheatleyGallery.com
E-mail: (insight@insightstudiosgroup.com)

Writer—Illustrator—Editor—Publisher

Mark Wheatley, Overstreet Hall of Fame inductee, has been awarded the Eisner, Inkpot, Mucker, Gem, Speakeasy, Golden Lion and nominations for the Harvey and the Ignatz. His work has appeared in Spectrum, the Library of Congress, The Norman Rockwell Museum, and other museums. He has designed for Lady Gaga, The Black Eyed Peas, ABC's Beauty and the Beast, and Square Roots, as well as Super Clyde, The Millers and 2 Broke Girls on CBS. His most recent print projects include Songs of Giants, Doctor Cthulittle, Tarzan and the Dark Heart of Time, Swords Against the Moon Men, The Philip Jose Farmer Centennial Collection, Mine! and Wild Stars. Past creations include Breathtaker, Return of The Human, Ez Street, Lone Justice, Mars, Black Hood, Prince Nightmare, Hammer of The Gods, Blood of The Innocent, Frankenstein Mobster, and Skultar as well as Tarzan, Baron Munchausen, Jonny Quest, Dr. Strange, The Flash, Captain Action, Argus, The Spider, Stargate Atlantis, Torchwood and Doctor Who.

WHITE, DAVID
Born—12 May 1965
904 Singer Ave.
Lemont, IL 60439
United States of America
E-mail: (davhite904@yahoo.com)
Writer—Editor—Comic Dealer

Lover of comics and pulps, started writing seriously about ten years ago, first published in 2012 with his original character Doc Panic. He has been published ten times and hopes to write way more in the future. He is lucky to have had friends like Tommy Hancock and Joe Gentile who pushed him to write and believed in him. The Pulp community both new and old has been a wealth of not only friendship but knowledge. Thanks to my wife Karen and children Brandon and Allison who have paved the way for me to be me.

YOUNGBLOOD, MICHAEL
Born: 10-23-70
Asheville NC
United States of America

Artist

I have a bachelor's degree in art
and I have done most of my work
in architectural illustration and
design. I have also done various
other freelance projects since
1991.

——

Art by Kevin Broden

Art by Brian Loner

APPENDIX A

NEW PULP PUBLISHERS

AIRSHIP 27 PRODUCTION
(http://robmdavis.com/Airship27Hangar/index.airshipHangar.html)

BLACK COAT PRESS
(www.blackcoatpress.com)

BOLD ADVENTURE PRESS
(https://www.boldventurepress.com/pulp-adventures/)

BRICK PICKLE MEDIA, LLC
(www.BrickPickleMedia.com)

CIRSOVA
(https://cirsova.wordpress.com/)

DMR BOOKS
(www.dmrbooks.com)

HIRAETH PUBLISHING
(http://www.hiraethsffh.com)

METEOR HOUSE PRESS
(http://meteorhousepress.com/)

MV Media—LLC
(https://www.mvmediaatl.com/)

ODD TALES PRODUCTIONS
(www.oddtalesofwonder.com)

PRO SE PRODUCTIONS
(http://prose-press.com/)

VALHALLA BOOKS
(www.valhallabooks.com)

WHITE ROCKET ENTERTAINMENT
(www.whiterocketbooks.com)

WORDFIRE PRESS
(www.wordfire.press)

NEW PULP MAGAZINES

PULP ADVENTURES
(https://www.boldventurepress.com/pulp-adventures/)

STORYHACK
(https://www.storyhack.com/)

Art by Clayton Murwin

APPENDIX B

WANT YOUR BOOK REVIEWED?

The following folks will read and review your astounding work. To find their links, sites etc. check out their individual entries in the book.

Ralph Angelo, Jr.
Chris Bell
Kevin Birge
David H. Blalock
Joe Bonadonna
Michael Brown
Adrian Cole
Dale Cozort
Pedro Cruz
Terry Crowley
E.W. Farnsworth
Thomas Fontenberry
Ron Fortier
Nancy A. Hansen
Rich Harvey
Greg Hatcher
Stuart Hopen
Michael Housel
Whitney Howland
R.A. Jones
Richard Kellogg
Rick Lai
William Maynard
Brad Mengel
Drew Meyer
Thomas Kent Miller
James Reasoner
Ernest Russell
Andrew Salmon
Brad Sinor
Arthur Sippo
Matt Spencer
Duane Spurlock
Jonathan Sweet
John Whalen
Michael Vance

"Rattler" sketch by Chuck Dixon

www.ingramcontent.com/pod-product-compliance
Lightning Source LLC
Chambersburg PA
CBHW081648270326
41933CB00018B/3387